Lihou Island

Never at Half Moon

First published 1989

Made and printed in Great Britain by
The Guernsey Press Co. Ltd, Guernsey, Channel Islands.

ISBN 0-902550-33-0

Cover design and artwork by Richmond Associates Limited,
Guernsey, Channel Islands.

CONTENTS

INTRODUCTION

Outside the Channel Islands, few people have even heard of Lihou, yet islands have a fascination for everybody and many, perhaps most people, have a secret fantasy about how lovely it would be, to be the sole inhabitants of a small island with nobody else to get in the way. Fairly soon, reality strikes when it is appreciated that it might be difficult to get the television repair man to call by boat, and even the doctor could be delayed. A few do make this fantasy into a reality and face up to the problems, but most of us put it firmly away at the back of the mind until Sunday lunchtime when we may listen to Desert Island Discs.

Many of our visitors tell us how fortunate we are, living here, which indeed is true, and we regard ourselves as the custodians of a magic island. Part of its magic is that Guernsey is the most populated Channel Island, but Lihou has one inhabitant for every ten acres and an unspoilt coastline of more than a mile. Nobody came to tell us how fortunate we were the day after the hurricane of October 1987 (nobody could come, the tides were wrong), but our first visitor was the builder coming to put the roof back.

People are aware that the biggest Channel Island is Jersey, the next biggest is Guernsey. Most could carry on and say that the next two in size are Alderney and Sark, but there general knowledge stops, except amongst those who have visited Guernsey. The next in size after Sark is Herm, which is actually the biggest island in a single tenancy. Sark and Herm lie between Guernsey and France, with two others, Brecqhou and Jethou, each of which has a manor house and some cottages.

The smallest inhabited Island of all is Lihou Island, which lies just off the west coast of Guernsey and has only one house on it. This is our home. We like to describe ourselves as living between Guernsey and Newfoundland, and whilst this is accurate one might add that we are only half a mile from Guernsey, but 2,249 miles from Newfoundland. It is usual to refer to our Island as Lihou Island, in contrast to the others, for instance nobody speaks of Alderney Island or Sark Island but "Lihou" is quite a common surname among Guernseymen, and there is a Route de Lihou and a Lihou House in Guernsey.

At the biggest high tides the Braye de Lihou, between Lihou Island and Guernsey is covered by thirty feet or so of water. At low tide the seabed is uncovered, and a Causeway appears, sometimes for four hours or more. At the smallest tides there is no more than eight feet difference between high water and low water, and the Causeway is never uncovered, so we are completely cut off for between three days and a week. I shall have more to say later (Chapter Seven) about the tides but the big tides occur at full moon and new moon, the poor tides at half moon, so we invite our friends, and the public, to visit us, but never at half moon.

Readers of my earlier book, *A Brief Guide to Lihou Island* may note that in the three years since it was first published I have been able to do further research and that I have corrected here some of the things which were stated incorrectly then. I have to admit that, like everybody else, at times I have made mistakes.

Neither my wife nor I ever visited the Channel Islands before the war, and it is a matter for regret that we did not know Lihou Island in the days when the very pretty previous house was still standing. We have been able to meet several people who lived and worked here and I am grateful for all the assistance I have received in writing this book. In particular I should like to mention Mrs Marie de Garis, Mr Hugh Lenfesty, Mr John McCormack, Mr Carel Toms, Mr Colin Best, Mr Victor Coysh, Mr Tom Babbe and his sister Mrs Margaret Piriou, Mrs Chloe Palm-Dekker, Mr Richard Heaume of the Guernsey Occupation Museum and Dr Warwick Rodwell, the archaeologist who excavated Les Ecrehous and has given me full access to his reports.

Acknowledgements also to John McCormack for his measured drawing of the Priory, and to Carel Toms, Tom Babbé and Chloe Palm-Dekker for the use of photographs, and Brian Green for his skilful enhancement of old photographs.

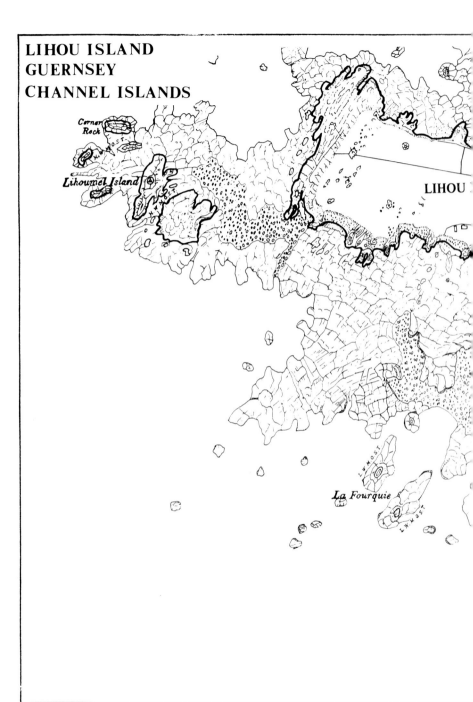

LIHOU ISLAND
GUERNSEY
CHANNEL ISLANDS

Corner
Rock

Lihoumel Island

LIHOU

La Fourquie

N

Lower House

High Water Mark of Ordinary Spring Tides

Lihou Causeway

Lissroy

THE CAUSEWAY

L' Eree

Low Water Mark of Ordinary Spring Tides

GUERNSEY

L' Eree Point

LIHOU ST

CHAPTER ONE
Early History of Lihou Island

Marie de Garis, in her comprehensive book *Folklore of Guernsey* has much to say about Lihou Island but here I should like to quote:— **"In Guernsey, the Catioroc headland and nearby Rocquaine beach have always been identified as the venue of witches meetings. A source of irritation and dread to the witch fraternity was the priory on Lihou Island, dedicated to the Virgin Mary. To the Mother of Our Lord they shrieked their challenge, shaking their clenched fists in the direction of the sacred fane. 'Tcheit, d'la haout, Marie d'Lihaou!' Fall from up there, Mary of Lihou! (It may be mentioned here that this little islet of Lihou has always been known to the country people and Guernesiais speakers simply as *Lihaou*, English pronounciation Lee-how, as opposed to the surname *Lihou*, pronounced Lee-who.)"** Today fewer people speak Guernesiais than formerly and Lihou Island tends to be pronounced as the surname.

All islands are interesting, some such as Volcano in the Mediterranean have acquired a reputation world wide. Islands are fascinating and always have been because they may disappear in the mist, and in ancient times many islands were regarded as being magic places for this reason. It follows that an island off an island must be specially magic, indeed many of them have been places of worship since the earliest times, and some still are.

Lihou Island is a very special lump of granite. Guernsey is another lump of granite, but there is a fault between the two, and geologists tell me that our lump is a little older — a hundred million years or so — than most of Guernsey. Many geologists have studied our rock, which is striated in several colours, with faults running across the Island, roughly north and south. There is some marble of no great quality and only in small pieces in both Guernsey and Lihou but no flint. Flint does however occur not very far out to sea and in quite shallow water, also it is frequently washed up on the beach.

The Channel Islands were certainly inhabited by Roman times and there is no reason to think that Lihou was then ignored by Guernseymen. There is a longstanding tradition that fishermen passing in their boats dropped their sails in salute to "the lady of Lihou", not, please notice "Our Lady of Lihou", which may point to earthmother worship here before the coming of Christianity. This tradition, Christianised, continued during the time of the monks.

Lihou Island may have been just a place to visit for worship, or it may have been inhabited by priests, priestesses or custodians of a cult, or indeed all three. The centre of worship, or of early habitation may well have always been near the site of the medieval Priory. There is a wall of large stones which runs in a straight line eastwards almost from the Priory Church to our sewer. This probably predates the Priory but its purpose is obscure. It is so close to the present coastline that in places it has been eroded away, but it is not in line with the coast or any other obvious point.

If indeed there was some form of Pagan worship here (as there was, elsewhere in the Channel Islands, for instance in Maitre Ile, in Les Ecrehous, as recent excavation has shown) we may enquire why this particular spot was chosen. Practically every religion in its worship employs some form of ritual washing (a parson today celebrating Holy Communion wears a vestigial towel on his arm, and consider the rite of baptism). Many forms of pre-Christian worship were centred on a water source, a spring or a well and people today who drop coins in a fountain might not like to admit that they are perpetuating an ancient Pagan practice. Whoever the first worshippers here may have been, resident custodians must have needed water for living, possibly visitors needed water for ritual washing of themselves and other rites. There is a natural water source on the other side of the Island (which dries up in the summer) called La Roche au Fontaine. Beyond Lihou lies another smaller island, connected to it by another causeway, this islet is called Lihoumel and has a natural rainwater pool. Surely, an island off an island off an island would be even more magic, and one wonders why neither of these two sites was chosen. There must have been water somewhere near the Priory, and I think I know where it was.

Worship in Lihou may have remained Pagan until the arrival of Celtic Missionaries in Guernsey from Wales in the sixth century, or there may have been a pre Celtic Christian place of worship, for the Celtic Missionaries were not the first Christians to arrive in Guernsey. If I am right in suggesting that there is evidence near the Priory of previous occupation, then it follows that the earliest Christians took over an existing site (with its well). By obliterating all or almost all traces of the previous users they would have "cleansed" the area and effectively prevented a recurrence of the previous form of worship. If the first use of the site was by the Celtic Church, then the same questions apply, and we must presume that these early Christians found water (was one of them a dowser?) and made a well.

It is probable that monks from Mont St Michel came here during the first half of the twelfth century. A document, since proved to be a forgery, dates the establishment of the Priory at 1114 but there is no reason to suppose that the date is all that far from accurate. Once again we are faced with the question, did the monks select a site on a previously

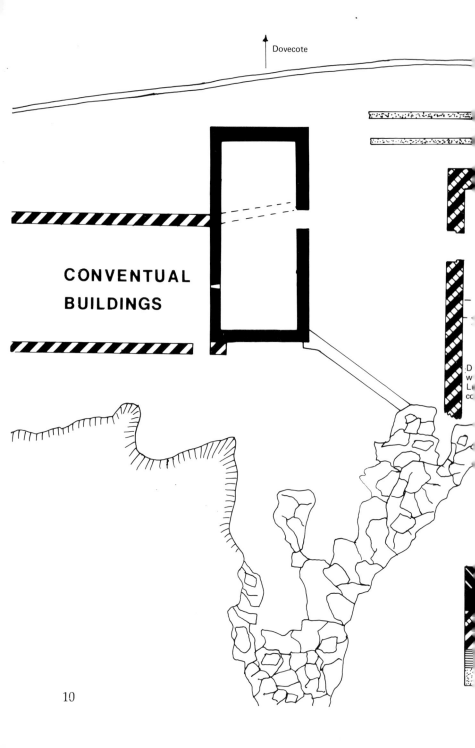

Dovecote

CONVENTUAL
BUILDINGS

D
W
L
cc

10

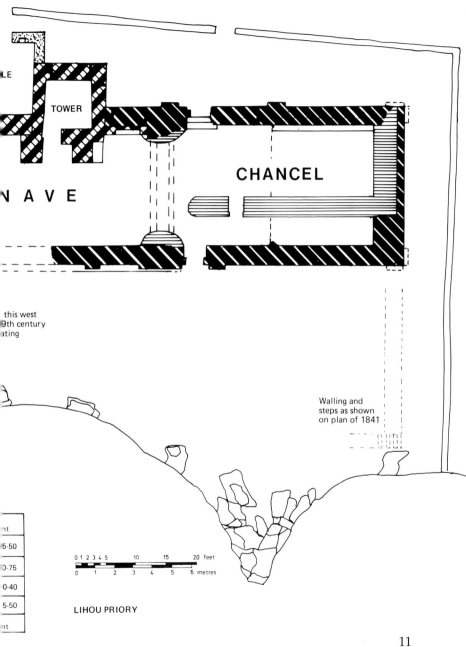

LIHOU PRIORY

unused Island (which seems improbable, islands only half a mile offshore are necessarily tempting) or did they come with the intention of taking over an island with a site of former worship, which had to be rebuilt to their own requirements?

There is a tradition that pre Christian worship continued even after the arrival of the monks from Mont St Michel. To quote Marie De Garis again:— "A tumulus at Le Catillon in St Pierre du Bois is known as La Hogue es Bringes (the mound under the brambles). The word Catillon itself means a small castle. It was probably a small defensive earthwork which once covered Rocquaine Bay. At the foot of the mound, there is a flat stone partially embedded in the earth. On it are marks resembling two footprints in opposite directions, as if two people coming, one from the north, the other from the south, had met on this spot and left the impress of their footprints on the stone.

There was once a hermit who lived in a lonely cave at Pleinmont. He was a very holy man and people made pilgrimages to seek his advice. He never left except to administer the Sacrament to the dying. He could be seen kneeling for hours at the foot of a Cross set upon the cliffs near the cave. One moonlit night a fisherman, anchored out in Rocquaine Bay saw him cross the sands of the bay and meet a tiny shrouded figure which came from the direction of Lihou Island. The two met on the stone at La Hogue es Bringes and stood talking together for some time. Then they parted, each returning back the way he came. Next morning the curious fisherman came to examine the place and found the imprints of two feet on the slab. He could not make himself believed when he told his story until it was discovered that the hermit had vanished. He was never seen again.

Another tale concerning the flat stone at Le Catillon is that once the *Dame* of Lihou and the *Dame* of St Brioc had a dispute as to the limit of their respective possessions. In order to settle the argument they agreed to both leave their respective houses at a certain hour very early one morning and walk in a straight line until they met. The spot where the meeting took place was to be considered henceforth as the boundary between the two seigneuries. They met here on this stone and both *Dames* impressed the slab with their footmarks.

Evidence as to the identity of the two *Dames* is very vague but the general opinion was that they were of fairy origin. *Dame* was one of the appellations of female fairies, especially if they were of higher status than ordinary run-of-the-mill *elves*. The religious of both Lihou Priory and the Chapel of St Brioc were male and so far as we know, no human women, *Dames* or otherwise were connected with them."

The second story appears even more confused than the first. A possible solution is that the Dame of Lihou is a representation of the Virgin Mary, but there is no reason to suggest that a Dame of Lihou or a Dame of St Brioc could ever have existed. The monk or priest or hermit is probably St Brioc himself. Standing or other remarkable stones were frequently used to demarcate boundaries between cults — or simply "civil" boundaries. A great deal of building, of development or redevelopment did take place in the twelfth and succeeding centuries for the monks were intermittently prosperous. We know that throughout Christendom in the Middle Ages the monks kept the knowledge of reading and writing largely to themselves and having a near monopoly of the subject, they kept records.

The Abbey of Mont St Michel kept the records of its daughter Priory. Later, at the French Revolution, the records of Mont St Michel, with its daughter Priories of Lihou and Vale (Guernsey) had to be deposited in the French National Archives — everything relating to Mont St Michel before 1789 went to St Lo, a city which suffered grievously during the fighting in 1944, when the archive was destroyed.

Well before the end of the twelfth century, the Priory Church had its vaulted chancel and its nave completed. During the thirteenth century the nave was vaulted and the tower was built at the north west corner. A fine building, if small, built from local granite with beautiful red granite (from Cobo, in Guernsey) for outer buttresses and doorways, this squared stone has been reused in other buildings in Lihou. By discovering as many of these stones as may be, it might be possible to estimate the height of the buttresses.

The Church was faced internally with Caen stone. This was imported, and probably carved on the site. There are a vast number of stone chippings on the foreshore, and it seems unlikely that the local vernacular stonemasons could have constructed a building to fit a ready made arch exactly. Were Guernsey stonemasons capable of carving quite sophisticated designs in a foreign material, or were men from Caen brought over to do this work? The church is near the beach, far from the highest point of the Island, but it is on top of a rise, and no doubt it was an impressive landmark viewed from the open sea.

Immediately to the west was a building in stone identified by Lukis as the refectory, where the monks would have taken their meals when in residence. If he is correct, he does not report finding more limpet shells here than elsewhere, although there are plenty on the shore nearby. Perhaps the monks were untypically tidy with their rubbish. Limpet shells were also used in the mortar, and it seems to me likely that the limpets were eaten first. Foundations of a further rectangular room, at right angles to it exist in the grass. The building which still stands above the surface was much later divided into two rooms, possibly a kitchen and larder, and the further room may have been the refectory itself. Nowhere so far has a hearth been found. The whole building could well have had an upper storey. There is no other building to be found which might have been the refectory. No evidence has yet been found to indicate whether the refectory or the church was the first to be built, but Le Patourel established that the further (westerly) room is earlier than the room still standing.

Dr Warwick Rodwell, in his excavation at Les Ecrehous, where the priory was established in 1203 has shown that there the main hall was built first, and it might seem logical for the builders to construct accommodation which they themselves could use before turning to the construction of the church. Here there is a space of several feet between the two buildings, so it cannot be said that one is tied into the other.

The only other stone building, or at least the only one of which traces are to be seen was the pigeon loft, on higher ground nearby. From this tower runs a wall which presumably was the boundary of the vegetable garden and would have been very necessary because the monks brought with them rabbits, then a rarity and a great delicacy. Monks have often been noted for a liking for the better (and perhaps more expensive) things in this life. The rabbits would have been originally in a fenced or walled warren, but in due course made their escape and colonised the Island.

Celtic monks lived in individual huts or cells, elsewhere often entirely constructed of timber, but here (where wood is not plentiful) normally of stone. To them, privacy and space for meditation was important. Beyond the refectory several circles may be traced in the grass, which may well be hut foundations. Roughly in the centre of these vestiges is one which seems to be usually, almost always, green and grows a lusher grass. This, I think, is the site of the well. One day we shall excavate it. There are various walls in this area, but erosion has taken its toll over the years, and some of them end where the beach has encroached, so does the drain. The Abbey of Mont St Michel was a Benedictine foundation (since the French Revolution Mont St Michel has been secular), and the followers of St Benedict have always believed in communal living. They would have wanted a dormitory, and even for two or three monks (and their servants) this must be a considerable building, but so far traces of it have not been found, unless, as I have suggested, it was in an upper storey of the 'refectory'.

The monks would not have been short of vegetables, always presuming that they had sufficient water for an extensive garden, and with meat in the shape of rabbits and pigeons, and plentiful fish and shell fish from the sea, life must have been worth living. The monks however went out to work in Guernsey, and it seems unlikely that many of them spent all their time or even much of their time in Lihou. Indeed, an article in the Proceedings of La Société Jersiaise in 1924 claimed that only two monks were "normally resident" but these may have rotated with others from the priory in the Vale (a parish of Guernsey).

By the mid-fourteenth century Lihou Chapel had fallen into disrepair and it needed to be rebuilt, probably on the original groundplan. Some Caen stone was re-used in the structure of the building, appearing eccentrically as the odd stone here and there amongst the granite. We do not know whether there was sufficient to reface the interior or even if more was imported at this time. The entire church was floored with green tiles, many of which survive. These are copper glazed on a buff clay base made in the south west of France and very similar to salad bowls and other pottery made there today.

14

The monks were far from being generally popular with the local people. They were believed to dabble in black magic and to practise Satanism. At least one murder occurred here (about the year 1304) when a servant of the Prior, Thomas le Rover killed a monk. The former Bailiff of Guernsey, Ranulph Gautier came to investigate and he killed Thomas le Rover. The Prior and monks fled to Normandy, and the Priory lapsed to the Crown. The monks were restored at least by 1347 when the *Garde des Isles* (the Governor) wrote to the King concerning the remuneration of the Prior. 1347 was an awkward time, the year of the Black Death and of the commencement of the Hundred Years War. Communication between Lihou Priory and Mont St Michel was difficult if not impossible.

There were times when the Priory prospered, and times of decline. In 1414 Lihou Priory (and all such priories controlled by foreign Abbeys) came under the financial control of H.M. Receiver General and remittances to Mont St Michel were alienated to the Crown instead. In 1415 the Priory was sequestered again, due to the hundred years war with France and it was vacant just at the time (1443) when King Henry VI was excited about his new Foundation, Eton College, then only three years old. He gave anything and everything he could to his college and one of these endowments was Lihou Island. Eton collected any revenues from it for a short period but the Abbey of Mont St Michel reclaimed it and re-established the Priory which then continued until the Reformation. As early as 17th July 1448 the Prior was summoned to Mont St Michel to answer charges of heresy, and to do penance. That Prior did not return to Lihou Island.

Another reason for the unpopularity of the monks, or if you prefer it, for the jealousy of the local people, was that the monks had the right of wreck, that is, the right to take into possession all driftwood and salvage. In the years between the end of World War II and the time when we came to live here in 1984, local people still used to come to collect driftwood, but now they are content to leave it to us, knowing that it is still to be found on Guernsey's beaches as well. In the days of the monks, before cargoes were containerised, the right to wreck must have been far more important. There was also trouble over the fish tithe. The monks complained that the fishermen did not produce the just amounts and only gave them the coarse fish. The locals said that when the religious insisted on accompanying them on fishing expeditions their catches were small — the old superstition that a parson on a boat is unlucky and brings small catches. The monks also had the right to vraic, that is the exclusive right to collect seaweed as a fertiliser from the beaches.

"Every Schoolboy" knows that the Reformation was prompted by King Henry VIII who wanted to divorce Catherine of Aragon and found the Pope unco-operative. Subsequently the King ordered the Dissolution of the Monasteries and took their fortunes and revenues into his own hands. That at least is one version of history. The Reformation was a vast popular movement across the whole of northern Europe and (although King Henry may have triggered it in England) it had to happen. Likewise, the Dissolution of the Monasteries was also inevitable because they were mostly nearly dead on their feet, and their treasure and estates were taken into the Treasury, to finance the country, not by King Henry personally. To take only one example, the vast Tintern Abbey in Wales had, at the time of the Dissolution, only seven monks.

Lihou Priory was similar, very few monks, perhaps no more than two and a Prior who lived (presumably in greater comfort) in St Peter Port. The Reformation and consequent Dissolution in fact hit Guernsey some thirty years late, when local Calvinists returned from Geneva in 1565. There was very little money and the monks, if any remained, went back to Mont St Michel. At the time the Prior was living in St Peter Port, and this could be because Lihou Priory had ceased to have anybody there at all. There is, in an old house at Perelle, a piece of beakhead moulding almost certainly taken from the Priory to make a laver or basin. This was probably in its new place before the Reformation. Local people are frequently accused (not only in Guernsey) of looting after the Reformation, but if the Priory had been abandoned some considerable time earlier, it is probable that building stone and other items of value were removed at that time. S. Carey Curtis, writing in the Report and Transactions of La Société Guernesiaise in 1913 quotes a reference to the appointment of a Prior in 1560.

The parallels between the Lihou Priory and Les Ecrehous are remarkable, but there Dr Warwick Rodwell has made thorough archaeological investigations. He shows Les Ecrehous as a prosperous community with several buildings, which then declined until only the church and the hall remained in use, and was then abandoned, well before the Reformation. He suggests that Les Ecrehous could have been finally abandoned following a natural disaster, inroads made by the sea.

If there were a natural disaster at Lihou I think it unlikely to have been a storm. In October 1987 there was a hurricane which struck Guernsey before racing up the Channel and hitting the south of England, but it hit Lihou first of all and took about half the tiles off our roof. It caused no damage to the ruins of the Priory, but that could also have lost its roof, if it had possessed one then. As at Les Ecrehous, erosion is a problem today, particularly in the area of the Chapel, and the sea gives us wonderful sections in the cliff as it wears away the clay. We always hope that we shall find something more interesting amongst the limpet shells and gravel which indicate the various layers of occupation.

My wife and I enjoy a daily walk around the Island (weather permitting), looking for driftwood and rubbish from the sea and in the season, mushrooms. It gives us a chance to check up on everything and see if there is anything which is not as it should be. Frequently, particularly after storms, we look at the cliff face near the Priory, where erosion frequently exposes a new section, usually with nothing more interesting than old winkle shells and traces of walls and evidence of earlier periods of occupation. One day recently my wife found a small diamond shaped piece of coloured glass sticking out from the cliff, more

than twelve inches below the ground surface. It was identical in size to the glasses one finds in a modern diamond paned window, but this was clearly very old, both from its provenance and its appearance. I posted it to the British Museum for assessment. The preliminary report reads:— **"I would have thought that the fragment of glass is certainly medieval — the condition, shape and grossed edges all point to this. I would suggest a 14th or 15th century date initially. There appear to be two lines at an angle to the general axis of the quarry and I do not entirely understand this."** A further report is promised.

Glass in those days was a very expensive luxury, and it is pleasant to have proof that the monks were wealthy enough to have stained glass in their windows, in the Chapel at least. When in due course it is returned from the British Museum it will be given to the Guernsey Museum, to join the finds from the Lukis excavation of 1838, which do include other fragments of glass (see next chapter).

Dr Rodwell relates that the chapel at Les Ecrehous was ruined by burrowing animals and that their digging made the south wall lean outwards. There Dr Rodwell suggests badgers in preference to rabbits but I do not know whether there is any basis for suggesting that badgers may have been present. The badger is carnivorous and would, I should have thought, found it difficult to survive on Les Ecrehous. I have not yet found evidence of any of the Priory walls here falling as a consequence of animal activity nor do I know (yet) how good were the foundations, but with so few monks (if indeed any were permanently resident) we may be certain that the rabbits proliferated and we may be also certain that they would have escaped from any enclosure in search of food. Rabbits normally live above the ground if there are few of them (as they did in England after the myxamatosis epidemic) and only go to ground when there is a population explosion as there usually is with rabbits. A rabbit, very sensibly, prefers to dig a burrow where the earth is already disturbed so it would choose a site between the Chapel and the Cemetery rather than the rocky ground in some parts of the Island.

Mrs De Garis quotes two poems about Lihou Island, one called The Trip to Lihou, 1595, the other The Voyage to Lihou, 1775. In each a parson takes some young virgins to Lihou, gets stranded, and out of the kindness of his heart keeps them warm through the night. Needless to say, by morning the ladies are no longer virgin. The first has an interesting preface, in which pre-Reformation Lihou is described:— **"It was famous for the superstitions practised by Popery. There were Monks and Nuns who lived there, devoting themselves to the Virgin Mary named Our Lady of the Rock and purporting to work miracles. The islet still contains a few remains of those times, part of a wall of the old chapel; there are also two huge caves hewed out of the rock."** It is certainly surprising to read that only some thirty years after the Reformation the Chapel was quite so derelict, and it seems more likely that only one wall had fallen. If indeed there were monks and nuns in the Priory no sign of a separate convent remains. The two huge caves hewn out of the rock are also curious. There is no trace of them today, presumably like so much else they have been lost to erosion. There is only one cave here now (not 'huge') which has been washed out of the clay by the tide.

The Church itself became a shelter for farm animals. The Church roof and maybe part of the south wall apparently fell down perhaps some thirty years later, and this I believe is the basis of the remarks in the preface to the poem quoted above. The Church is not big and the nave is not wide, but still too wide for the farmers using it to span with a new roof. Their solution was to build an intrusive wall along the length of the building making it narrower. The builders of this wall did not hesitate to re-use carved Caen stone in its construction and they left an entrance or doorway in it. No doubt it was effective and what remains of it shows that it was substantial, but one cannot help thinking that repairs to the south wall as necessary and a proper roof spanning the whole building would have been less trouble and more useful. Turning once again to Les Ecrehous there the chapel was converted to secular use after the departure of the monks, and the evidence for this consists of traces of fires lit on the floor. No such evidence is recorded here and unfortunately the floor, or much of it, has been removed in recent unqualified excavations.

The refectory and the dormitory above (if this is what the monkish arrangement was) were probably used as accommodation by the shepherds and other farm workers who attended at Lihou Island occasionally in post Reformation years. A curious outhouse was built on to the north-west corner of the church and then extended by two walls close together pointing towards the 'refectory', perhaps some sort of external furnace. This building, often mistaken as part of the Church, is in fact early nineteenth century, and is usually marked on archaeological plans as a "stable", but it is clearly too small for such a purpose.

CHAPTER TWO
The Middle Years

The two Bailiwicks of Jersey and Guernsey are ruled each by their own **States** but decisions of the States have to be endorsed by the King or the Queen (as the case may be) by Order in Council. Three Orders in Council dated 1737, 1847, and 1849 each mention the "Three Islands" which are Erme or Herm, Jethou and Lihou. All of these were, until 1946 Crown tenancies or leases and the Orders in Council lay on the Lieutenant Governor of Guernsey the responsibility of leasing them. In 1946, the freehold of Herm, then being untenanted was sold by the Crown to the States, who have since been at liberty to include it within the civil law of Guernsey, and to find their own tenant at a rent fixed by them. Jethou has been on a normal limited lease since 1860 or thereabouts, but the lease for Lihou Island is most unusual.

From the Reformation until 1737 leases were signed in respect of each of the "Three Islands" limited to the period of office of the Governor. This could only be uncertain and unsatisfactory for the tenants. In 1737 leases were signed to take the three Islands as fee farm holdings. The lease for Lihou Island is still written for sixty one years, renewable after twenty one years. Our lease may still be bought and sold, but only with the approval of the Crown, and the tenant has to be the holder of a British passport. For about forty acres of not very good farmland, and inaccessible as well, one can only say that the rent, by the standards of the time when the lease was written is exceptionally high, but it cannot be altered. It is £3.8s.6d (now £3.43), per annum. In 1847 the Crown attempted to raise the rent (hence the Order in Council) but this was shown to be *ultra vires* and corrected by the further Order in Council two years later, in which the Crown agreed never to vary the rent, provided the lease was renewed.

During the later part of the eighteenth century and the Napoleonic Wars the safety of the Channel Islands gave much concern. The Channel Islanders had once been French, or at least, Norman. Guernsey French was then the normal everyday language. Some perhaps of the population might have had some sympathy with a French invasion. Strategically, the Islands were unimportant, but as a propaganda factor the loss, and the gain could have been immense. Lieutenant Governors determined to take steps to minimise the danger. The French fleet could land soldiery in Lihou Island prior to an invasion of Guernsey. This would in fact be good tactics, an invader needs to occupy outlying islands first, to prevent pockets of resistance. The Lieutenant Governor ordered that the Priory Church and refectory be blown up to prevent their use as a French barracks. He could not have been visualising a very big invading force. The church was already something of a ruin, and much remained of it subsequently, but there is no doubt that very considerable damage was done.

Circular defensive towers were built all round the coast of Guernsey and their siting was duly appreciated by the invaders when eventually invasion did come, in 1940.

One barracks, Fort Richmond, and two of these towers, Forts Grey and Pezeries (Pleinmont) command the approaches to Lihou Island. Fort Saumarez, on L'Erée Head, the nearest point in Guernsey to Lihou Island, dominates it. Originally Fort Saumarez was not very high, and is one of three true Martello towers built in the local granite (the others are Houmet and Grey). Most people (myself included) have thought that Martello Towers were designed by a military engineer of that name but this is not so. In 1794 a Royal Navy force, consisting of three ships of the line and two frigates planned an assault on a tower at Cape Mortello. 1,400 troops were landed, and a combined attack was made. One ship was set on fire and lost over sixty men, killed or wounded, and another was forced to retire after two and a half hours. Eventually a lucky shot from the shore force set the tower on fire and the garrison, when it surrendered, proved to be only 33 men. Whether the British regarded these towers as being almost magic, or simply very formidable, they had no doubt that the design could not be bettered, and immediately a rash of them was built along the south and east coasts of England and in the Channel Islands. Perhaps there is something magic about Mortello, or as everybody now calls them, Martello towers, not one has ever been assaulted or captured. In accordance with military practice, it had a separate shed or *magazine* for storage of gunpowder and other stores and this had a ridge roof to avoid lodgement of fireballs. Extraordinarily, it is so close to the main tower that a lucky shot could easily have rolled down the roof and stuck between it and the tower.

Had Fort Saumarez been built to a sufficient height, it could have commanded the whole of Lihou and its approaches. This was not done, and a watchroom was built here instead. There are several things I would like to know about this watchroom, particularly why it was built on the second highest point of the Island in such a position that it was still possible to approach from the west, unobserved. Presumably a watchman or watchmen lived there the whole time, ready to flash a lantern if an invader was seen and it must have been lonely to be there for several days, a week or more, cut off by the tides. One hopes he had a reserve lantern, in case the main one blew out. This watchroom was built to a standard design, and was identical to several in Guernsey. The military specification laid down that these watchrooms were to be built in the

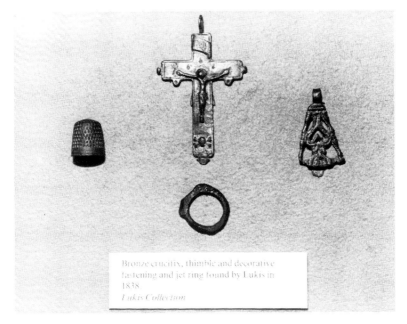

Bronze crucifix, thimble and decorative
fastening and jet ring found by Lukis in
1838
Lukis Collection

finest Guernsey granite, so the stone was carried across the Causeway.

In 1815 a Royal Commission reported that Guernseymen were claiming to themselves the right to vraic*, which properly belonged to the Crown as the inheritor of the monastic rights formerly enjoyed by Lihou Priory.

In 1838 an archaeologist named F. C. Lukis was active in Lihou Island. He came of a well established family. The first Lukis recorded as settling in Guernsey was a soldier in Captain Lyttleton's company of Cromwell's New Model Army, sent to Guernsey during the Civil War. He came from Cornwall which was (like all the West Country, particularly the rural areas) a strongly Royalist area. His parents did not forgive him, so he stayed here, and later, after the war was over, he was joined by his sweetheart, a girl named Dorothy Cooper, also from Cornwall, and one can only presume that she loved him enough to make a hazardous journey probably in a fishing boat. F. C. Lukis had many descendants, some of whom went to Australia and some back to England, but today there is only one with the surname Lukis still living in Guernsey.

By the standards of his time F. C. Lukis was a good worker. He wrote a proper report, and his finds are today in the Guernsey Museum in St Peter Port, including a fine bronze Cross dating from only shortly before the Reformation. It is in remarkably good condition, and museum

*vraic (pronounced rack) is the local word for seaweed. Compare the English wrack, as in seawrack.

21

reproductions of it have been made for sale. Lukis also excavated around the building which he identified as the refectory. Some trenches which were dug either by him or a later archaeologist are still to be seen today.

He starts his report by telling that he and his family** (apparently his wife and three daughters, aged twenty and two teenagers) **"repaired thither, and occupied the house, which was then comfortably fitted up by Mr James Priaulx who enjoys the fee farm tenure of the Island."**

I interpret this as implying that Mr Priaulx had only quite recently completed construction of the house. Lukis gets quite poetical in places, describing **"The Isle of Lihou, situate on the west coast of Guernsey and on the verge of ye Atlantic Ocean . . . a safe and quiet place for the residence of a Prior, or as it has been said, of an Abbess and her nuns."** Unfortunately he does not say by whom it has been said, and I can find no firm evidence that there were ever nuns in Lihou Island. The Priory was dedicated to Notre Dame, (the Virgin Mary, also known as Our Lady) and it may be that this is another confusion between "Dame" and "Notre Dame".

I have been given a copy of an extract from a letter from Lukis to a friend, Lt Col H. Smith, at Plymouth. This was found amongst the papers of the Guernsey Society, which exists to serve the interests of Guernsey-men overseas. Nothing further is known of this letter except that it is written from "Grange" (which is in St Peter Port) and dated October, 10th 1838.

"My original plan was for the examination of Druidical Remains, so that I have delayed entering into those of more recent date, but will also form the next object of research. I should, however, state that finding myself residing for some weeks in the Isle of Lihou, "La Sainte Isle de Lihou", we cleared a great part of the church and priory there. In one room we found about 20 coins and also much tracery and orna-mentation of the church. This place must have been handsome and contained more carved work than any existing church in the island. A mass of steel and iron denoted armour. This we found in a small chapel adjoining and might have been armour deposited in the place, or hung up near the roof. This of course would fall with the stone roof which was found to encumber the whole of the interior. The destruction of this building was doubtless by violence and not by time. The dedication of this church bears the date 1117, but I conceive from the examination of the spot that like most of our churches there stood a chapel or religious house on the spot. The work is now suspended but I hope to resume it next year."

The same sheet of paper contains this note:—

"A piece of green porphyry was found in Lihou and was cut into three parts and made into silver-mounted brooches for Lukis' three daughters — Louisa, wife of Rev. Wm. Thos. Collings, Seigneur of

**Although he states that his family accompanied him, in fact only his three daughters did so. He also had four sons.

Sark, Mary H. Mansell Lukis and Margaretta Sarah, wife of Rev. L. Astley Cooper."

The coins are now in the Guernsey Museum but I can find no trace of the steel and iron and it seems curious that he should have found anything in the Church resembling armour. I do not know what he meant by "a small chapel adjoining". It might have been the base of the tower, or Lukis may not have realised that the wall running the length of the nave was a post-reformation insertion, and there is nothing on the plan to indicate that he appreciated this. Indeed the plan shows the northern portion of the nave as "CHANCEL or Lady-Chapel".

Perhaps he meant the area between it and the original south wall, which on his plan is designated "South Aisle". Certainly he could not have meant the stable which is so labelled on the plan and which is only delinated by a light dotted line. In any case, as we know by traces which still remain and by Mr Dekker's photography, the "stable" had a roof of pantiles and Lukis specifies a stone roof.

Lukis was aware of the fact that the Priory was blown up by order of the Lieutenant Governor, as he mentions in his report. The speculation that "The destruction of this building was doubtless by violence and not by time" is therefore curious. The date 1114, mentioned in his report was taken from La Dedicase des Eglises, a document which has since been proved to have been a forgery, although this particular date may perhaps be described as informed guess, not too far out. In the same Dedicase the Vale Church (which is mentioned in the report) is attributed to 1117 and this may have been the reason for misquoting this date in his letter.

The note appended to this extract from a letter is unsigned and undated. The Collings family held a mortgage on the Seigneurity of Sark from Mr Le Pelley, the previous Seigneur who started a silver mining enterprise under the sea off Sark. This was a disaster which resulted in the deaths of several miners and is still remembered in Sark today. It bankrupted him so in 1852 he was compelled to surrender the property to the Rev. Wm. Thos. Collings' mother who was by then a widow. She became the Dame of Sark and was succeeded by her son as Seigneur. The Rev. Wm. Thos. Collings was Seigneur of Sark from 1853 to 1882. Mrs Hathaway, the redoubtable and famous Dame of Sark for many years including the period of the Occupation was his granddaughter. The present Seigneur, Mr Michael Beaumont, is her grandson. The note on the letter therefore must date from 1853 or later.

So, apparently, must the final version of the archaeological report, for in it Lukis relates the finding of the porphyry:—

"In removing a tile on the same side of the Chancel there appeared at a depth of a foot beneath it a piece of porphyry and the bone of a human toe. Both these appeared as having been placed there for conceal-ment. The stone bore marks of having been once polished and cut by the saw of the lapidary. The exterior edge bore the semblance of having had small fragments there of chip off with design. This relic which is

23

of Egyptian green porphyry resembles some of the stones of the same kind, which are found in the mosaic patterns round the shrines of Saints abroad. Similar portions of the same material are still to be found round the Tomb of Queen Eleanor in Westminster Abbey.

This stone was of sufficient thickness to be cut into three parts, and form three broaches, (sic) which were mounted in Silver, with the annexed inscription and presented to my three daughters, who were present at the discovery, viz: Louisa Elizabeth Lukis, now the wife of the Revd William Thomas Collings, seigneur of the Island of Sark, Mary Ann Mansell Lukis and Margaretta Sarah Lukis now the wife of the Revd Lovick Astley Cooper, M.A. son of Sir Astley Paston Cooper Bart. of Gadebridge, Herts (vide sketch and inscription)."

Louisa married her cousin in 1847, nine years after the excavation.

The sketch is there, and in the margin are two notes, one reading **vide plan of Chancel at X** but unfortunately X has been omitted from the plan and the other reading in different handwriting **The fragments of Egyptian green porphyry were cut into Seals by John W. Lukis 1838.** John W. Lukis was one of Louisa's brothers, two years her senior. I do not know whether, like the original finisher of the stone he was a 'lapidary' or merely an amateur.

Louisa's brooch has been passed down in the family and remains the property of the present Seigneur. Mary Ann never married and her brooch is in the Guernsey Museum. Margaretta Sarah apparently went back to England with her husband but now the present head of the Astley Cooper family has no knowledge of her brooch. Clearly, although the three brooches could not have had much intrinsic value, they were at the time much treasured in the family.

Lukis' original plan was for the examination of Druidical remains. By this he must mean traces of pre-Christian, pagan worship. Whilst I believe that this was indeed such a site it would be interesting to be able to discover what made his think so. Later archaeologists have concentrated on the Church which is certainly the most dramatic part of the ruins but so much remains to be done.

Lukis presumably drew his ground plan and sketches on the site, or one of his party did. The ground plan is unsatisfactory. There is no scale, and I doubt (although I have not measured it on the ground) if it is in proportion. There is no distinction between walls which are tied in and contemporary and those which have been built later and butted on. In the refectory, an internal wall, which is clearly an insertion placed at an angle across the room is drawn as if it were a part of the original structure and shown as being square. It did not appear to worry Lukis that all three rooms are shown with no doors at all and only one window between all of them.

It is not unusual to find an archaeologist writing his report some fifteen years after the excavation. A modern excavator might ask "What, only fifteen years?" and we may presume that he made notes on the site at the time. We know from his letter that he intended to return the following year but do not know why he did not. Probably he did write some preliminary report whilst it was fresh in his mind but this has not survived.

To anyone interested in history it is a source of pleasure to know something of how much archaeology remains to be done. So far, archaeologists here have mainly concentrated on the church, although a little work has been done on the cemetery. It would be fascinating to excavate a complete skeleton and to find out what the deceased had eaten, and how old he was, perhaps even the cause of death or at least traces of some diseases suffered in life. Also largely undisturbed are the conventual (or domestic) buildings, particularly the foundations of the Celtic huts.

Mr James Priaulx in his long tenancy did more perhaps for the Island than anyone before or since. He built a very fine well proportioned house of three stories, large enough for himself and family and for some workers. A lintel from his period survives incorporated into the garden wall above one of the gates. I do not know whether this was its original position. An inscription decorated with rather primitive rosettes reads:— J P. 1834.

In the 1840s Europe experienced a population explosion, which was partly the result of the industrial revolution and partly contributed to its success. In some countries, real distress was caused by the pressure of people, and one country which was ripe for disaster was Ireland. In 1846 potato blight struck, in the English west country, in Wales and much more seriously in Scotland. Ireland suffered widespread starvation in a time which has become known as the Great Famine. The principal causes were lack of communication and lack of education even regarding such elementary matters as the use of flour in lieu of potatoes, and the use of fish from the sea. Facilities for the distribution of relief supplies of corn were poor. One of the British Government's solutions was to provide free or nearly free transport to Canada for Scotsmen and Irish who could no longer scratch sufficient living for everybody from their meagre land. Some of the Scotsmen went south to North Carolina in the U.S.A. where their descendants still live (and talk American with a Scottish accent) but most went west in Canada to the Rocky Mountains which reminded them of their native homeland. Most of the Irish went southward to the U.S.A. (anything to get away from Canada, part of the British Empire), but some, perhaps less adventurous, went no further than Guernsey.

Mr Priaulx employed Irish girls in Lihou. Later, girls here were to be frowned on as a possible distraction for the workmen. In those days the main language in Guernsey was Guernsey French, which differs materially from Jersey French and is enough to make a purist Frenchman hold up his hands in horror. The Irish speak English which is grammatically excellent but these girls probably came from the west of Ireland where the potato famine caused the greatest distress and their accents proved hopelessly unintelligible to the Guernseymen who referred to them, and their language as Anghlais Patate — potato English.

Mr Priaulx enclosed a considerable area around his house as a garden, with plenty of outhouses and he sank a well for water. He formed a business selling vraic as a fertiliser in Guernsey. Lihou Island has always been notorious for the vast quantities of seaweed deposited during the season on its beaches.

He used the watchroom as a two storey cottage for a farmworker and it has since always been known as the Upper House. I have not been able to find there, any trace of a well, which indeed one would not expect on high ground, so water would have had to be carried up to it, nor is there any sign of a cess pit, so presumably there was no more than an outside privy. The watchroom apparently had been a cottage in effect since the Napoleonic wars, replacing the accommodation in the Priory blown up by order of the Lieutenant Governor.

Sledges with cart horses were used to remove the vraic from the beaches, and Mr Priaulx had ramps cut to each beach. These may still be seen today. The vraic was transferred to carts with wheels and carried across the seabed, then to all parts of Guernsey. In moving the very heavy vraic from Lihou Island to Guernsey he encountered a big snag. The load had to be very full to justify the cost of delivery, but a full load was too much for a horse up the rough sandy track over the beach. He paved all the hilly parts of the Causeway. We still do not know why he chose to take such a twisty route, perhaps it has always been the best and flattest way across. What we do know is that it has stood the test of time and no amount of rough seas appears to move those granite setts. We did, in 1985, have to replace the last three courses with concrete where the paving ends in the centre but as far as I know that was the first maintenance needed in a hundred and forty years. It seems that the centre portion of the Causeway was never paved. The slipway on the Guernsey side is earlier, probably 18th century, but it has later patches, some of which are repairs of wartime damage.

Mr Priaulx also laid gravel along the tracks where his horses were going around the Island. Today the gravel has long been covered with turf, but the grass grows much shorter and finer over the gravel, making a firm and pleasant path for walkers and a good surface for the occasional trip by tractor or car around the various parts of the Island. Most of the very well built field walls (which are pointed with mortar, not dry stone) were done in his period, but there are also some later subdividing walls. Sadly, all these walls suffered during the war and to rebuild them today would be quite uneconomic.

The waters surrounding the Channel Islands have always been notorious and numerous shipwrecks have occured. One of the most dangerous parts is the west coast of Guernsey where the sea is shallow and rocks, some concealed just below the surface abound. Wise sailors stay at least three miles out from this shore. During the first Great War a British ship with a cargo of coal was caught by a German submarine out to the west of Guernsey. The U boat commander behaved punctilliously, giving plenty of warning and time for the crew to take to the boats. In those days life boats were equipped with nothing more efficient than oars and the U boat started to give the lifeboats a tow towards Guernsey. The commander then apologised saying that he had been told on his wireless that he must go and sink another ship so they were left to row for the shore. Plenty of people were waiting to rescue them by the time they reached Lihou Island, but one member of the crew at least, who had lost his bearings said that he had understood that the Isle of Wight was much bigger and not nearly so close in to the Mainland.

About the turn of the century the vraic acquired a greatly increased importance. In those days the only effective wound dressing known was iodine, and an immense quantity was used. Iodine is obtained from the ash of burnt vraic and the whole of the garden of the house became a factory, with racks for vraic outside and a furnace. An old Guernseyman, who once worked in the iodine factory told me that between four and eight horses were employed here during the season. It was a prosperous business until a double blow fell about 1935. In South America a new process was invented which enabled iodine to be sold at a price which greatly undercut any produced by the old method, and in California a new oil well was sunk, where the main impurity proved to be iodine, which had to be taken out to sell the oil, and therefore was (in the oil company's eyes) obtained for free and to be sold for what it would fetch. Lihou Island reverted to being a farm.

In most of the interwar years the owner of Lihou Island was Mr Freddy Best whose son Colin is still a local farmer. He repurchased from the executors of Mrs Southall those fields at L'Eree which were once in the same ownership as Lihou Island. They are naturally flat land, and were Guernsey's original airfield (abandoned as being too small before the war). His farm is still known locally as the Aerodrome.

We have been fortunate in meeting one elderly gentleman, Mr Bretel, who worked in the iodine factory, and also Mr Tom Babbé and his sister Mrs Piriou whose father was the manager. Apparently the vraic was first sun and air dried, then burnt in a furnace with forced air. Mrs Piriou recalls that it was very hot near the furnace. The residue was then put into big cisterns under the outhouses and soaked. These cisterns are still there, no doubt by the end of the war they were full of rubble but the outhouses were rebuilt as garages and when we came all they needed was a good scrub. We redirected the rain water from all our roofs into them. There are four of them, of 1,500 gallons each.

The liquid from the cisterns was distilled with permanganate in a retort, and the resulting crystals were bottled and dispatched to England. The ash was thrown in the area of the Priory cemetery, and future archaeologists may well be confused by finding it there. I am told that earthenware jars labelled LIHOU were used to convey the iodine to "somewhere up north" (I have not yet discovered where) and these jars were returnable. One or more of them could have survived, and I still hope that one day we may happen upon a jar and return it here.

The manager was Fredric Henry Otto Babbé, a native of Antwerp,

27

known here as George. He saw the world as a steward with the White Star Line. On a visit to Guernsey he fell in love with it and took a job as head waiter in a local hotel (the Gouffre Hotel). In due course he met and married a Guernsey lady, a trained nurse and they had five children all of whom still live in Guernsey. He had to give up a cottage belonging to the hotel when he left that job.

During the summer school holidays (which were four weeks) Mr Babbé would take the young Tom for a fortnight in Lihou, then his brother Peter went for the second fortnight. The girls were allowed visits by the day when the tides permitted, and sometimes one of them might be allowed to spend the weekend there, after the workmen had gone home. Mrs Best, the owner's wife, did go there with her husband frequently, and so did their terrier Floss, who was a champion ratter. Mr Babbé normally came home for the weekends, either with a horse and boxcart, or by using the flat bottomed boat across the passage. Fred the horseman did the rowing and Mr Babbé and Tom did the bailing with old cans.

The owner, Mr Freddy Best, also had a factory in the Steam Mill Lanes, St Martin's, in the south of Guernsey. Mr Best is remembered today as a man who did not see why he should not use his car during the Occupation, just because the Germans forbade it. He painted the car in German army colours and drove around as he pleased. The German soldiery, knowing that only officers had cars, always saluted him.

Mr Babbé was quite an inventor, experimenting with iodine. Apparently his most successful product was called "Salvador", a remedy for eczema,

George Babbé.   *Young Peter Babbé with Floss.*

and Mrs Piriou tells me that people still remember it and bemoan that it is not now available. According to Tom Babbé, there were then four working horses kept here permanently, their names were Prince, Champ and Cognac, and one other. The horseman was Fred Savident, who (in young Tom Babbé's day) was in his seventies and according to Tom an old character. He was as strong as a lion and he could pull nails out of timber with his teeth. Surprisingly he had a complete set in spite of the way he used them. Modern toothpaste manufacturers would be horrified to know he never used the stuff, but we do not know whether he had halitosis. There were also pigs, and in the summer, young heifers. The flora of the Island included scabious and orchids. We still hope they may come back.

As late as the early 1930s, women and girls were discouraged in Lihou Island. We have a copy of a photograph (perhaps dating from the turn of the century) of a young woman raking the seaweed into the furnace. Her name is said to be Mrs Le Riche, the only woman then apparently allowed. Far from distracting the men, they lean idly against the wall watching her at work. Only the dog shows any enthusiasm to join her.

One of her successors in the early 1930s was a man living in the Forest (a Guernsey parish about five miles away). He walked to work every day in all weathers, presumably crossing by boat when he could. Many people today would consider the walk there and back in itself sufficient exercise, but at least he was doing work which previously had been thought not too strenuous for Mrs Le Riche, who, to judge by the photograph, was not an outstandingly muscular woman.

Conditions in those days must have been primitive, with no electricity. The house was infested with fleas, and the Island with rats. It was usual for Floss to dispatch a couple of hundred rats in a weekend. Lihoumel, the small islet beyond Lihou Island was known in those days, at least to the Babbé children, as Rat Island.

When we arrived, the house had not been lived in, but a caretaker spent occasional nights in the cottage at the back. He may not have **been careful about disposing of food waste, and certainly there were many rats (but no fleas) quite near the house. Once they knew we were there all the time the rats quickly found other accommodation elsewhere in the Island, but we have done all we can to keep them under control and now there are very few of them** — certainly no dog could find two **hundred, or anything approaching that number.**

Today, there are fourteen entries in the local telephone directory of people with the surname "Babbé" so the late George Babbé could be proud that so many of his descendants have stayed here.

In 1922 there was a sensation in Guernsey when a very large whale was washed up in Lihou Island. Guernseymen cut it up with cross cut saws. A large pit was dug in Lissroy, and the bones and other remnants buried there. The whale was said to be over sixty feet long, and the pit was nowhere near as big, so the carcase must have been considerably reduced before burial. The pit remains today, a shallow rectangular depression.

Mr Priaulx may also have made the large pond on the Lissroy peninsula, at the southern end of the Island. Old photographs prove that this was in existence at the time of the iodine factory. I thought originally that it indicated the water table, but this is not so, it almost dries up in a rainless summer but water is available elsewhere. Fairly certainly, it was constructed by laying clay in a natural hollow and I think it was the principal source of water for horses and cattle.

By 1945 or so iodine had effectively been superseded as a wound dressing by other, better drugs. One of several objections to it was that its application caused painful stinging. Today it is required, in much smaller quantities for drugs in thyroid disorders and in some dyeing processes.

I am told that before the war barley was grown in the higher fields of Lihou but so near to the salt spray it seems unlikely to me that it can have been of good quality. Another crop was mangolds. Apparently also young heifers were kept here, growing on.

CHAPTER THREE
Recent History

Farming was not a prosperous industry in the nineteen thirties and by 1939 nobody was occupying the house at all, even on an occasional basis, but the then owners of the Island (the Best family) came over for summer picnics with the children. A gentleman from the Netherlands called Willen Frederick Dekker rented the house as a holiday home. He first came to Guernsey some years previously, and walked across to Lihou Island. On the Causeway he met a local girl, Miss Enid Ruth Webb, and subsequently they were married, so there was a very strong sentimental attachment to the Island. They brought their two sons, Herbert Reginald and Lancelot to Lihou Island for summer holidays, but did not return in the summer of 1939, the year that their daughter Chloe was born.

One of the sons now lives in U.S.A. and the other in The Hague and Chloe, now Mrs Palm-Dekker, also lives in the Netherlands. She came on a holiday to Guernsey recently and I was delighted to meet her. This was her first visit, and she brought with her photographs taken on holiday by her parents (who of course are now both dead). Today's house is very different to the one she knew from the photographs but the ground plan is the same and I was able to show her where some of the pictures were made (and she took new photos of the same places). The house was apparently then known as St Mary's Priory House. Chloe has kindly given me permisson to copy some of these old pictures for this book.

Imagine the fun that we had when the new enlarged copies of these old photographs arrived and we went round the Island trying, mostly successfully, to identify the places. The rock named by Mr Dekker as the Profane Prior proved quite easy, and indeed at the correct angle, particularly when he is covered up to his middle by the advancing tide he looks quite convincing. The place called by Mr Dekker, John Thomas Beach was less easy but the triple rock in the background proved that we had found the right place. The views at the front and back of the house were informative, and we had not previously seen an oblique view of the front, showing how big the iodine factory buildings (and particularly the building with a chimney) were. Comparing the picture of Mr Dekker with his pony and traditional cart with the other, earlier, view of the house when the iodine factory was in its heyday shows that

already by about 1938 some of the shacks and racks outside the garden wall had been removed.

One of the most exciting photographs proved to be one of a not very interesting door with a carved keystone above it. This is in fact the 19th century "stable" attached to the Priory Church. Only a fragment of the pantile roof remains today, and there is no trace of the lintel. This was made of wood, little more than the top piece of the door frame and it is not surprising that it has disappeared, either as the result of bombardment or simply rot. Anyway, I recognised the keystone, and found it again. It was a piece of Caen stone, undoubtedly originally imported to be a part of the facing of the Church. When we first saw it, we put it down as a fake, perhaps carved by some of the young people in the holiday camps, yet here it was, in a pre-war photograph. Today it is chipped and smaller but the important part is intact. I await expert opinion on the question of whether it is in fact an earlier fake, carved in the 19th or early 20th century. Presumably S.M.D.L. means Sainte Marie de Lihou but the mortar surrounding it in the photograph is paler, and looks as if the stone was probably a later insertion. There could have previously been an arch (traces of what might have been arch springing may be detected) and we just do not know what was the purpose of the shed or stable. It has a fireplace in one wall, with an outside forced draught, so it could have been a forge for the repair of machinery. Certainly nothing was wasted in making it elaborate, so I presume that the stone was probably to hand and was placed there at some time, just for fun.

One Guernseyman told me that he was a boy in 1940, and he came to Lihou Island on the day the Occupation started. He found an interesting carved stone and hid it in the bracken. After the war he searched for it, but was unable to find it and presumed that some German soldier had taken it home as a souvenir. It seems to me unlikely that any German (even an officer) would have been permitted to carry anything as heavy in his baggage and this may be the stone which he found.

Another photograph, equally exciting for us, was captioned as being the Priory, but initially we were unable to place it. It was John McCormack who identified it for us. There is a painting (I have only seen a reproduction) by Joshua Gosselin (1739-1813) dated 1793 which shows the ruins of the Priory, then standing about twenty feet high. This picture shows two blind arches which do not exist today. An undated photograph shows a lady and a gentleman standing in the ruins with the same arches in the background. To judge by the costume, the photograph dates from around 1920. By then the back wall of the larger arch had disappeared and the remains of the church tower may be seen through it. The outside walls of the church were somewhat reduced but still much higher than they are today. Mr. Dekker's photograph proves that these arches were still extant in 1938, although the walls had further tumbled to some extent.

In preparation for war, the British government had planned to evacuate all children from London and the major cities to "safe areas". In view of what happened less than a year later, it comes as a surprise to find that the Channel Islands were considered (but not used) as a possible

safe area. The fall of France was so sudden that many people living here found it difficult to believe, and although ships were sent to evacuate the population, some did not see the necessity of leaving. Those who stayed woke up on the 30th of June, 1940, to find their Islands under Nazi occupation.

There will always be debates as to why, having ejected the British Army from France at Dunkirk, and captured most of its equipment, Hitler did not cross the Straits of Dover immediately. In the event, England was not invaded and the only British territory occupied was the Channel Islands. Hitler believed that this would hurt British pride and that every effort would be made to recapture them. In fact the British were chiefly concerned with leaving the Islanders in as much peace as possible and not causing unnecessary bloodshed. However, Hitler built his "Atlantic Wall" (which proved useless in 1944, as the Maginot Line had in 1940) and nowhere was it stronger than in the Channel Islands. Surveyors attached to the Occupation forces looked at the forts and towers and found them well sited, but Fort Saumarez was not high enough. Therefore a field gun (that is, a gun on wheels, fully mobile) was taken to Lihou and some of the rock on the highest ground was blasted to make a site for it. Today the rocks there look like a mouth with a front tooth missing. The gun crew was lodged in the house.

Vast military engineering works were performed throughout the Channel Islands, and one of these was to extend Fort Saumarez upwards, and to build concrete trenches and pillboxes around it. These still remain, and Fort Saumarez looks a little peculiar, but it cannot be denied that the architecture "makes a statement". The tower was a lookout point only, a captured French tank was sited on the platform beside it and other guns were placed near the other towers and forts. Four captured Russian 16 inch guns were placed on the higher ground further back. They were apparently so big that before firing practice soldiers had to go round the local houses warning the people to open their windows.

It was no longer necessary for the soldiers to visit Lihou nor possible for anybody else. The whole coast was mined and covered with barbed wire to prevent the Islanders escaping, or commando raids from England. Lihou was used as a target. That is the reason why today it is pock marked with craters and very occasionally unexploded shells are still to be found. The house was nearly razed to the ground, and the Upper House (which had anyway been disused since the iodine factory was abandoned) was ruined. The Occupation forces were ordered to leave the Priory alone, whether this was obeyed or not, it is certain that it was hit at times, and perhaps we may be charitable and suggest that some of those behind the guns needed more practice.

It is said that in the middle of the war a Spitfire ditched in the sea off Lihou Island and the pilot swam ashore there. Skindivers have claimed to have seen the wreck. According to the story, the pilot walked unobserved to L'Erée Head, fortunately not setting off any of the mines.

He was befriended by local people who wanted to hide him, but he appreciated that if he were found, the Occupation forces would take his hosts to a labour camp in Europe. To avoid this, he gave himself up and became a prisoner of war. I have given the details of this story to R.A.F. Records but they unfortunately were unable to trace the pilot, who is reputed to have come back to Guernsey in recent years for holidays and may well be still alive.

After the war, Guernseymen wanted all traces of their horrible experience removed and so guns and other military ironmongery were taken away fairly rapidly. The Channel Islands remained littered with concrete and it seems unlikely that any of this will ever be cleared. A claim for compensation was put in on behalf of the Bailiwick of Guernsey (and settled) but in calculating it Lihou Island was forgotten.

A syndicate of English people led by an estate agent called Mr F. B. Conniff bought Lihou shortly before the war intending to build an hotel but they were defeated by the water problem and never got beyond the planning stage. I do not know whether the plans still exist. In 1952, Professor and Mrs John Le Patourel camped in Lihou Island and did an excavation at the Priory. They were the first post-war, and so far the only archaeologists to dig here scientifically and present a proper report. They point out that most archaeological sites in Guernsey are situated in urban places which have subsequently been built over (a common problem) and that Lihou Priory, never having been a site for redevelopment is now the most extensive monastic area to be found in the Channel Islands.

The Le Patourels intended their excavations to be extended over a period of years but in the event they did not return after 1952, and they deserve credit for having completed and published their report. It appears not to have struck them that there might have been occupants before the Benedictine monks, but they were interested in the conventual (domestic) buildings and examined, dug and reported on the refectory building as well as doing some work on the Church. They also mention that Major Carey Curtis did some excavation in the Church and published his report in 1913, but I have not read this.

The Island then lay, empty and ignored until it was bought by Lt-Colonel P. A. Wootton in 1961. At that time no work had been done since the war. The house and the old iodine factory lay in ruins and I regret that if photographs were taken then none have apparently survived. Col. Wootton had homes in Sussex, in Malta and in Guernsey so he had plenty to occupy him and it is not surprising that he took some time before he got round to rebuilding the house here.

Col. Wootton bought, with the Island, a stretch of waste land overlooking it and extending to about two acres, up to and including the Tower. Below the Tower on the far side there is a house called Fort Saumarez and the then owner asked Col. Wootton to sell the Tower to him. The Colonel obliged but the remainder of the land was sold freehold to us when we bought the Island.

The Colonel caused the hardcore of the iodine factory to be bulldozed into the lower part of the garden and found the well which had served the pre-war house under the rubble. Within a day or two of taking possession of the Island we hired a JCB tractor and driver and had it scoop out all the rubble from the lower garden and deposit it over the edge on the beach. Some of our friends enquired whether we were not satisfied with what we had bought and were trying to make the Island bigger. He repaired or rebuilt the boundary walls and new garages on the site of the old outhouses. As he planned it, the house was to be his retirement home, and it was built to the same ground plan as the old house, re-using the old granite. The old house had a wing jutting out to the back, dingy kitchens partly below ground level. Here he built a separate self-contained flat in 1966 and the Wootton family lived in it on their occasional visits to Lihou Island until the main house was finished in 1978. The flat has only one bedroom and a living room, plus a kitchen and bathroom, so it must have been fairly cramped, even as a holiday house, for the Wootton family with three small children.

In 1966 Col Wootton decided to issue his own Lihou Island stamps. Gibbons Stamp Catalogue is rather snooty about such issues:— **"Local carriage labels and Private local issues: many labels exist ostensibly to cover the cost of ferrying mail from one of Great Britain's offshore islands to the nearest mainland post office. They are not recognised as valid for national or international mail. Examples: Calf of Man, Davaar, Herm, Lundy, Rabay, Stroma. Items from some other places have only the status of tourist souvenir labels."**

In fact he had a precedent. Herm had a sub post office from 1925 until 1938 when it was closed due to lack of business. The first postwar tenant of Herm, Mr A. G. Jefferies applied to have it re-opened in 1948, but this was refused because the population was too small. Mr Jefferies then took to carrying mail on behalf of the residents of Herm to Guernsey in his own motor boat, and charged for the service by issuing his own stamps. There was no telephone in Herm in those days, and Mr Jefferies instituted an air mail service on 26th May 1949. No aircraft can land on Herm, and this is the only instance in modern times, at least as far as I am aware, of a genuine pigeon post. It was not long lived, the pigeons went into retirement on the following 30th September when a telephone was installed. The surface mail continued, and every letter posted in Herm had to bear a Herm stamp as well as the appropriate British stamps.

The same considerations hardly applied in Lihou. At the time there was no permanently resident population here at all (even the Colonel had homes in Guernsey and elsewhere), and no pigeons. Tourists had no need to post their letters here, and indeed we get thousands more now than ever came in his day and none asks for a posting box. However, whilst Stanley Gibbons description of "tourist souvenir labels" is fair enough, I think they might also have been described as a little bit of fun which did no harm to anyone. Col Wootton had been punctillious in obtaining the permission and approval of the General Post Office.

The General Post Office was changed into the Post Office Corporation on 1st October, 1969. At the time, both the Bailiwick of Jersey and the Bailiwick of Guernsey established their own independent post offices and U.K. stamps were no longer used in the Channel Islands. Nor were carriage labels from offshore islands to be allowed. Some four months before the Guernsey Post Office became operational a law to that effect (involving a possible fine of up to £500, never as far as I know, invoked) was passed by the States. Col Wootton was bitter about this law, at least partly because he had recently ordered a new supply of stamps which had cost him money to have printed.

That there was at the time bitterness is not in doubt, indeed Col Wootton has said as much. He caused comment in the local paper and a Parliamentary question in the House of Commons.

Whilst Lihou stamps were superfluous and possibly could have been confusing to post office sorters, there is no doubt that they were sought by stamp collectors. Some fifteen years after they went out of circulation a dealer in St Peter Port found some (including first day covers) at the back of a drawer and asked us to sell them for him. We had no difficulty in finding buyers and even today we have one or two letters every year from stamp collectors (often from Germany) enquiring whether Lihou stamps are still current and whether we can supply them.

In 1974 a small cargo ship, the "Prosperity" was wrecked off the west coast and much of its cargo was washed up in Lihou Island. Unfortunately for the Guernseymen the cargo was not whisky but it was still well worth having. It was in fact timber, but the local people behaved as the Scottish islanders were depicted in the novel and film *Whisky Galore*. Col. Wootton, perhaps remembering the ancient right to wreck enjoyed by the monks, claimed it for himself and in consequence found he was resented much as the monks had been. Later, the Commissioner for Wrecks, acting on behalf of the Crown and the Salvage Association acting on behalf of Lloyd's Underwriters, the true owners, went round claiming any timber they could find, but unfortunately no Guernseyman who was thought to have collected any timber could remember where he had put it. Years later (1987), my builder, inspecting the damage to the inside of the roof after the hurricane had no difficulty in finding and identifying some of the timber. It had made very good rafters.

By the time that the main house was completed, the Colonel had already started to have an interest in Canada. He had plans, not realised, to build a wind generator in a tower, and to build a place of worship near the Priory. One of the things which he did here, and for which he is most remembered is his introduction of Ronaldshay sheep. This breed from a Scottish island is on the list of rare breeds and is chiefly notable for the fact that they will eat seaweed, if nothing better is available. The flock here was not attended daily, and were very wild, but they multiplied, and when we bought the Island there were more than eighty of them in only forty acres of poor pasture. Col. Wootton was unable to catch them and unable to sell them, so he abandoned them to us. We

39

sold them to a farmer in Guernsey and since then the grass has recovered and wild flowers which had not been seen for many years have returned.

I think that he would regard his Lihou Island Fellowship as his greatest achievement during the time that he owned Lihou. It consisted of a couple of holiday camps lasting a fortnight each in the summer for teen-agers, mostly living under canvas. The camps had a strong religious flavour, and he would interrupt activities at regular intervals for prayers. Various activities were offered to the campers, such as botany and meteorology and rock climbing. A very popular activity was archaeology. Each activity had a Leader, and he appointed himself Founder and Chief Leader. His camps were continued for several successive years.

The archaeology was mainly examining and lifting the tiled floor of the Priory Church, and digging small holes below it. Unfortunately some digging was done too near the one remaining half arch of the nave which was the highest part of the ruins and was known to be unstable. No harm was done at the time but the following 27th December (1979), when nobody was present in the Island, this wall fell. It remains as rubble on the ground, and will not now be moved until a qualified archaeological team is ready to excavate beneath. Another project is to remove the wall built about 1590 along the length of the nave, for under it will be a portion of the church undisturbed since then.

Lihou Island has always been an attractive place for Guernseymen to visit, and when we lived in Guernsey my wife and I used to come here occasionally, just to walk and enjoy it and to see the seabirds. By the time Col. Wootton put it in the hands of estate agents we knew it well, but of course we had never been inside the house. Perhaps we did not realise it at the time, but already we loved this Island. I suppose the correct answer to that comment is that every Guernseyman does.

We did not come to Guernsey planning to live in an outlying Island, and Lihou was the only one which appealed to us. The house in which we were living previously was exceptionally pretty, in a deep sheltered valley surrounded by trees, but we found it cramped. When we bought Lihou Island all our friends told us we were mad, and we tended to agree. Privately, we were worried by the enormous amount of work which needed to be done, but we set out on a great adventure.

CHAPTER FOUR
Taking an Arkful to Lihou

There was much curiosity among Guernseymen as we completed the purchase of Lihou Island on the 1st November 1983. We had not lived for long in Guernsey and were not well known, so people speculated about what we were going to do with it, whether we would spoil it, and would we place any restrictions on public access. A certain amount of cynicism greeted us when we said that we looked forward to living there, and several friends said that they would give us six months at the outside. Less cynical than most, the local Rolls Royce agents invited us to a party, and to test drive their latest model. Unfortunately it is not a fourwheel drive car, and a little big for crossing the Causeway.

Right from the start, we announced one new restriction. We did not intend to allow dogs in Lihou. We knew that this would lead to some disappointment from people who had always exercised their dogs here. We were accused of being dog haters. We are not, and indeed we have our own dog, but we are bird lovers and we did not want them disturbed, also, we know that even if they are asked, or required, to keep their dogs on a lead some will not do this ("Rover is so good at following"). We wanted to avoid dog fights. Whilst a few people complained, a much larger number congratulated us, saying (which had not occured to us) that it is a pleasure to come to Lihou, which is clean under foot.

Our predecessor sold licences to shoot rabbits, and very considerable slaughter took place, several hundreds, or thousands, a year. To the regret of the shooters, although we honoured licences for 1983/4 sold before we owned the Island, we have refused further requests and it is our opinion that the Island is thereby made more peaceful. We were told that without shooting to control them the rabbits would proliferate. Nowadays there is much more grass and other vegetation here without the sheep, but the rabbits have not multiplied beyond their previous level. The rabbit population varies from year to year but when there are too many Nature adjusts itself and the litters are smaller.

I have been surprised to note how very territorial rabbits are. At some time in the past a domestic rabbit has been released, and near the house there are several white collared rabbits. Near the Upper House there are black ones, but they do not appear to interbreed, I have never seen a black rabbit with a white collar for instance, and they keep to their own tight little areas. Tom Babbé (see Chapter Two) told me that fifty years ago the black rabbits used to live around the Priory, but I have not seen any there.

At the time when we bought the Island, Guernsey was entering a temporary and quite short slump in property values. Apart from bargain hunters, we had no serious buyers looking at our house in Guernsey until the following mid summer. We had to continue living there, keeping it up, and coming across for a day or two when we could. There was a great deal to do to the house in Lihou Island, involving virtually complete redecoration, and some alterations. When the tides were right, carpenters used to come over on an early morning tide, work eleven hours and go home in the evening. They were up on their luck, under contract to work forty-four hours and doing a week's work in four days. We moved as much of our furniture as we could, mostly by the car and trailer, leaving our Guernsey house still looking lived in, and we stayed here whenever possible.

Zelda, our saluki, and our two cats always came with us in the car and when we were going to be here for a night or more we let the cats loose. Both cats were Maltese born (and had spent six months in quarantine). They had lived with us in our small house and garden in St Martin's but when they arrived here although they had never seen a rabbit before they knew instinctively how to hunt and found fresh meat preferable to what comes out of a tin. It is interesting to note that a baby rabbit, like an unweaned kitten flops when picked up and carried by its mother and that the cats kill sufficient rabbits to eat (but no more). When they catch a baby rabbit they bring it in, alive and unconcerned, and then do not know what to do with it.

At last we signed a contract to complete the sale of our house in July 1984 and in the middle of that month we moved. We used two removal vans, and a couple of farm tractors and trailers to carry the heavy stuff across the Causeway. It was all done in a day. Mid July and there had been no rain for weeks. Needless to say, that day the heavens opened (as the weatherman had predicted) but the removal men had forgotten their polythene sheets.

The previous day we had moved my pet horse Rashid. He is a grey gelding, foaled in 1969 and I have owned him since 1972. He was born in north Africa, a countrybred arab, and in his youth was drafted into the Libyan Police. Whether he did not like the Libyan style of riding I do not know, (he still carries spur scars on his flanks) certainly he has always been afraid of bangs (the only thing which frightens him) and this may be the reason why he was cast from the Police. He was put in a boatload of horses for Malta where I bought him. He travelled to Guernsey after us when we left, by ship to Marseilles then overland. On the day when we brought him to Lihou Island he walked across the Causeway led by me with no trouble, but on the following day Mr Colin Best was going to hold a horse show on his land at L'Erée. The car park was full of Jersey horseboxes camping overnight and the horses

were whinneying. It was more than Rashid could bear, and he tried to walk across the Causeway at high tide to see if he had any friends there. It is a mistake he has never tried to repeat. Rashid is always pleased to greet everybody who comes here, and visitors have suggested to me that if he could talk he would work as a guide to the Island, and probably be a great bore.

Fortunately, the outbuildings are excellent, and there was little to do to make the stable ready for Rashid before the winter. It had never been used for livestock before, but it did have a divided stable door. Besides Rashid, we had moved with ducks, bantams, our cats and Zelda the dog. Unless and until we could find a competent islandsitter we could not leave it. Patricia's mother was seriously ill and she had to go and attend to her frequently, but I was not to spend a night anywhere except in Lihou Island (sometimes alone) for eighteen months.

We were of course delighted to be sleeping for the first time with our own bed in our new home, knowing that we were certainly the first people to do this without a home in Guernsey since the war at least, and historians agree almost certainly since the Reformation. At any rate, nobody has so far suggested that any previous owner of the Island lived there full time. We knew that our problems were only beginning but we had no idea what they would be.

We erected a notice at the far end of the Island, proclaiming that Lihoumel (that small group of rocks beyond) which is a separate island at high tide (and several islands at a very high tide) is a closed bird sanctuary. People respect this notice and the seabirds are not disturbed.

43

The way across to Lihoumel is rough, the rocks there are slippery and it would be easy to fall and break a leg. I do not want the job of rescuing anybody suffering an accident, nor do I want people to get themselves stranded there.

All my life I have been interested in donkeys, we ran a most successful donkey stud in England for years and Rashid always had at least one for company when we were in Malta. He and I were sad that we had none when we lived in Guernsey, and he would always whinney a greeting whenever we passed one in a field or on the road. A donkey mare named Lollipop joined us from Jersey soon after we came to live in Lihou, with her foal of the year. She was already in foal again, and has since been back to Jersey on another visit to get in foal once more. Of course a donkey foal is a most attractive animal, and her foals have come in for much petting by visitors, and a few titbits. All our animals have learnt to pose nicely for photographs, but I am afraid that I had to laugh on one occasion when I saw a tourist running backwards (fortunately not near the beach) trying to get far enough away from Lollipop to get a photograph. She was convinced he had something for her.

Her most recent foal, Poppadom, had to be dragged, almost carried, protesting across the Causeway, when, one day short of a year old we found a new home for him. Both we and Lollipop were fed up with him by then, only Poppadom considered he was marvellous. On the Causeway he told everybody that we were cruel taking him away, that he did no want to leave the Island and above all he did not want to leave his mummy. At L'Erée Head, still protesting he was loaded into a horsebox and taken to a far part of Guernsey. His new owner has two fields, each side of a valley and separated by a *douit* (small stream). Her own two (female) donkeys had been put in the further field and Poppadom was let loose in the nearer one. He ran down to the stream, jumped it and announced, loudly, that he was much happier being a great big grown up donkey and did not want to return. He has not given us another thought.

At times we are asked whether we provide donkey rides. No, we do not, and Lollipop has no intention of starting. She is happy being everybody's pet and meeting visitors, but neither she nor we wish to start that sort of work, nor does the Island need it.

Buying our annual supply of hay is always interesting. It comes by tractor and trailer and usually gets bogged on the beach. Sometimes we have to off load the hay there and bring it in our own vehicle up to the barn. One year it was delivered on a short tide, and had to be dumped, below high tide mark, for us to pick up and stack as the tide came in.

One day we found a young fantail pigeon, crouched in the long grass, and very tired. In the past we have kept fantails, which are very decorative and no trouble. We caught this one, and caged it for a month. During that time we were able to acquire another two pairs from a farm in Guernsey (their owner was only too pleased to have his stock thinned). They settled and started breeding very soon. I do not know how many pigeons we now have, nor could I recognise our original stock in the flock.

We have informative notices for our visitors, with pictures of the sea birds which may be seen here. One tourist asked us what were the white birds grazing together on the Island which were not illustrated, they looked just like white pigeons. Another pointed out (correctly) that we did not include peacock amongst the wild birds to be found here. One of our notices carries the logo of the Royal Society for the Protection of Birds, because the R.S.P.B. representative arranged for it to be given to us. It was a present from Mr James Thomas, owner and manager of the Guernsey Zoo. Lihou Island is a bird sanctuary by our own choice (including the land we own in Guernsey I think it may be the biggest in the Bailiwick) but it is maintained by ourselves and we have no other connection with the R.S.P.B. apart of course from goodwill. Occasionally the local branch arranges a visit here for its members, and their young ornithologists (as nice a bunch of kids as you could meet anywhere) come twice a year or so.

During the spring and early summer we have to rope off some parts of the Island where birds are nesting, to avoid people walking on the nests. One man objected to this, telling us that he, his father and grandfather before him had always walked around Lihou and we were not going to stop him now. Further, he added, our chickens and ducks were more of a menace to the wildlife than he was. He told us that there were now more notices in Lihou than there had been during the Occupation. This seems likely, as nobody was allowed here in those unhappy days, so there was no need for notices. At least I hope that those that we do have (far fewer than formerly) are both polite and informative.

However, one Scottish gentleman ignored all our notices and the ropes intended to keep people away from the nesting seabirds, and when we remonstrated with him, he told us that the "Holiday Special" publication stated that "visitors are welcome to roam all over the island" and he intended to do what it said. He later posted a cutting to us to prove he was right, and we were thankful that he had not wanted to roam around our bedrooms. Another recent visitor also deliberately passed the notices and stepped over the ropes. When I went to speak to him he thanked me for putting up the notices forbidding admission to the breeding grounds, it made it so much easier for him to find the nests and examine them. How fortunate we are that such people are very rare, at least as far as we are concerned, and most of our visitors are entirely delightful.

Our ducks provide much amusement, both for ourselves and for our visitors. They also give us a few eggs, but mostly they are rather secretive about this. We have some plumpish lavender muscovies, and more mallard than we know. All of them are very greedy and they, and the chickens, come round begging for food as soon as the visitors arrive. We now sell small bags of corn for the children to feed to the ducks. The corn may be maize, or wheat or a mixture. We once watched in amazement, so did the ducks, as a boy of sixteen or so bought a bag of maize, sat down and ate the lot himself. One distraught Mum telephoned after a school party had been here to say that her darling moppet, aged six, had eaten a bag of wheat. This is not recommended, but it did no harm. She was, we gather, told not to do that again.

Children who come here in the summer enjoy picking up the chicks and the ducklings and provided they are very young when first picked up they do not mind at all. (Those who do object are quite capable of taking evasive action). It seems to us that, particularly for town kids, it is a thoroughly good thing to have an opportunity of handling animals and the parents enjoy photographing them. So far, we have had no complaints about soiled clothing.

For a long time we wondered why people were buying bags of corn and taking them away unopened, then we discovered that one highly intelligent mallard duck had hit on the idea of flying away to the car park and begging round all the cars. People go there for picnics, or to admire the view, simply because it is so delightful whether the Causeway is open or not, so there was often some bread or something for her. Many people thought she was a stray and starving (I am not sure why, she certainly did not look it), and even the corn merchant, making a delivery to me was taken in by her. Sometimes she took her drake over with her. When the evening came and the cars left she flew home to us for her supper.

The peacocks are a great attraction. We are lucky that we have no neighbours who would suffer damaged gardens, and object to the noise that they make. In fact happy peacocks who are free to roam seldom make much noise, outside the breeding season. In their first year here we were unfortunate, we did not realise that peacocks are not strong fliers, and that they would go down in the winter onto the beaches. We lost them both in a storm. Now we have several but they have to be caged from September till April. The hens make nests in the bracken well hidden in remote spots and appear with a clutch of babies in June or July.

One of our peacocks was a gift from a widower who was going to live in Portugal. He also asked us to look after his four geese, whom he had kept for several years. I made it clear that I did not need any more geese, but was prepared to accept them. He brought them the next day, when he released them they were very wild and ran away. Then he told us that they were not less than twenty eight years old. They soon became tame, and the three survivors eat out of people's hands. One of them has actually laid eggs and gone broody, which is quite an achievement at her age, even though she has not yet succeeded in hatching live goslings.

CHAPTER FIVE
The Island and Us

We had heard from our predecessor that the well was excellent, that it had never dried up. I am sure this was true as far as it went, but of course it did not occur to us that he had only lived here for a maximum of two weeks at a time. Certainly the well is beautifully built, lined in brick and perfectly circular and plumb.

The summer of 1984 and the previous winter had not been very rainy, and it did not take long for the well to run dry. We had the last drop of water analysed. It was beautifully soft but it contained lots of interesting minerals (no gold or silver or platinum) of which the biggest concentration was lead. Silver is to be found, so geologists tell me, under the seabed between here and Pleinmont, but to mine it would not be economic. Memories are long in the Channel Islands, and with the terrible disaster which struck offshore miners seeking silver off Sark in the mid-nineteenth century, nobody wants to try. We were recommended not to use the water from the well for any purposes involving cooking or drinking by people or livestock.

Tom Babbé has since told us that the well always dried up in the summer, and water had to be carried across. With all the people living here in the heyday of the iodine factory, the work horses and perhaps young cattle as well, this must have been a considerable undertaking, particularly as it was necessary to have sufficient water to last seven days when the tides were bad. The season for making iodine was of course when the vraic piles up, and it may be a solid wall up to four or five feet high and perhaps thirty feet across. At such a time the Causeway is impassable with a modern four wheel drive car so it cannot have been easy to take a horse drawn watercart across, yet this was the time when the population of the Island, people and horses, was at its greatest.

Until we solved this problem we took to bathing in the sea (fortunately it was summer and quite warm) then rinsing the salt off in a water butt in the garden. Modesty was not a problem, we were alone on our Island, loving it and prepared to laugh, (but sometimes a little desperately) at almost anything.

A dowser (water diviner) came to see us, and recommended a borehole not three feet away from the well. Good water, he told us, would be found at a depth of one hundred feet. The well is thirty feet deep.

The only drilling rig in the Channel Islands lives in Jersey, but often comes to Guernsey. On its next visit it trundled up the Causeway and started work where the dowser had told us. There was a little water in the well and we watched with interest as the drill reached and passed a depth of thirty feet. There was not a ripple and we were left in no doubt that this bore had no communication with the well. At a hundred feet water was found in very small quantities, and the drill went on. At 108 feet water was plentiful and we could stop. Of course we need a powerful electric force pump to bring it up, but there are a dozen 100-gallon header tanks in the roof, giving us sufficient water for normal domestic use at all times, and the pump works if needed when we switch on the generator.

At the time we had staying with us a young man who was working for a degree in geology. Various people over the years have studied the geology of Lihou Island, but nobody had been able to go beneath the surface. His thesis includes details and samples of the rock to a depth of 108 feet, and this fresh research helped to earn him his degree.

Col. Wootton, when he first started rebuilding here bought a second-hand generator, an old Lister diesel. When we arrived it was already more than thirty years old, and we were told that on one occasion, before the generator shed was built he left it outdoors through the winter and it needed extensive derusting and repainting. He had expected it always to start first time, even when he had been in Canada for six months, and was not disappointed. A fine old machine, it served us faithfully for three years, but eventually it had to be replaced. The generator shed had been built round it, but fortunately the doorway was wide enough to pull it out. Bringing the new one across the Causeway and manipulating it around to the door (which is on the far side of the generator shed) was not easy. Before I bought the new one, I obtained an estimate from the States Electricity Board for mains power. It would need a trench cut through the granite of the Causeway for half a mile and they were not prepared to say how long that would take. The cost would have been in excess of £50,000 but there would be a bonus, I could have a free mains water pipe laid at the same time. We had no difficulty in deciding that this was quite uneconomic.

I sold the old Lister generator for a small sum to a Guernseyman whose hobby is remaking old machinery. He knew what was wrong with it and why I had found it to be beyond economic repair. It left here on the back of a tractor and for all I know he may well have put it right and it may be working now and good for another thirty years. I wish him luck with it.

I spent much of the first winter in Lihou pulling down rusty old barbed wire, whenever it was not raining or very cold. The wire had been put up, unstretched, apparently to try to keep the sheep in, but even if one liked barbed wire (I hate it) the fence was entirely ineffective, mostly broken, wound round with brambles and overgrown with thistles. It had been hung from wooden posts sunk in concrete, which I pulled out with a tractor. Taking down two or three hundredweight of barbed wire does not sound too big a job, but in this case it then had to be loaded into a trailer and taken across the Causeway to a skip in the next village. Now we have only short wooden fences, on each side between the garden wall and the sea. There is a stile for people and a gate for animals and vehicles in each. None of our animals has wished to escape and go to Guernsey so our neighbours do not find their gardens disturbed, and the animals take full advantage of all the grass available.

The agricultural tractor which we first had here was not entirely satisfactory and we obtained instead a secondhand builder's dumper, an unsprung four wheel drive vehicle with a large container or bucket in front for concrete, sand or anything. Before it was delivered we were asked whether we would like the bucket removed and replaced by a seat, which I could only describe as a throne, so that I could drive across the Causeway with Patricia sitting in front in state. In fact, the bucket usually carries an oil tank for fuel deliveries. The dumper is far from elegant but it does have a personality of its own, and whilst it has rather more rust today than it did in its youth it is a most reliable old friend which has never let us down.

Before we moved we knew that transport was going to be a problem. We had a very neat little car, ideal for Guernsey's narrow twisty roads, but we sold it and bought a four wheel drive car of land rover type (Japanese in fact). The first one was noisy and not very comfortable and so affected by rust caused by sea water that we had to sell it within three years. We replaced it with something called a Fourtrak which has proved entirely satisfactory and much more comfortable and is guaranteed for six years against rust. It also has a very useful winch, which comes in for all sorts of purposes as well as being there should the car get bogged. Many people ask us how our tyres stand up to the Causeway, but this appears not to be a problem, the tyres on our first car looked like new even when the chassis was long past its best.

It did not prove easy to find the right people to live with us, sharing our home and the work of the Island. For a few months one summer we had my niece, Amanda, my brother's youngest daughter, then aged twenty. A thoroughly energetic girl, a real country lass who would not feel lonely when the tide came in, or yearn for the bright lights (which may be seen, across the sea, from here). She went about the work of the Island, smiling and laughing, but never stopped talking. On one occasion we did find her speechless. I had sent her out, as the tide started to cover the Causeway, to tell some people who had just arrived to turn back at once or they would be stranded. "Oh that's all right, dear," she was told, "we're getting off at the other end." We never have worked out a suitable reply.

For a long time we had nobody, and when it became essential for both of us to be away together we just had to ask friends to come and stay as island sitters for a few days and look after the animals.

In 1987 we decided that the time had come to accept that Lihou Island was more demanding than we had first thought, and that the two of us were insufficient to manage it alone, particularly as Patricia's father, by then a widower, wanted to take us with him on holiday trips. We advertised for staff, and had many replies, most of them hopeless. One applicant wanted to know whether there was a choice of schools in Lihou for her six-year-old daughter. Before we were able to interview any of the people we heard from our friend Les Dunford.

Les and Anne Dunford owned their house in Holmfirth, next door to where the television programme *The Last of the Summer Wine* is filmed. They had heard that we were looking for somebody and thought that quite apart from anything else, the weather in the Channel Islands was better. (Little did they know about the hurricane which was to strike, but not in Yorkshire, only a month after they arrived). This house is bigger than we need, and they fitted in perfectly. There are also two small bedrooms for their daughter, currently at university and their son Jonathan, who now lodges in Guernsey and goes to the Grammar School.

Moving the Dunsfords from Yorkshire was in some ways more of an epic than moving ourselves just from Guernsey. They had less furniture (but quite enough) and the only animal involved was Lizzie the black cat, who looks so like our Natasha that they are impossibly jealous of each other. Les hired a large van and brought it over on the ferry. Quite the biggest and most interesting piece of furniture was Jonathan's organ which is an instrument of considerable weight.

The organ had been the last item to come out of Les's hired van, so it was the last load which the dumper tackled before the tide came in. Carefully we put the dumper under the roof of the woodshed, to protect the precious organ if it rained. For the next couple of days Les was busy arranging his furniture and the organ stayed in the dumper. I had some shopping to do and I took the car to Guernsey, but there was rather a lot of seaweed on the beach and I was hopelessly bogged. I could not get the car out with its winch, because there was nowhere to attach it on the open beach, Les went and fetched the dumper to pull the car out. Several visitors asked whether he always kept an organ in the dumper but he pointed out that it is not equipped with a radio. We were moving it through the door (quite a vigorous exercise for the three of us) when the cuckoo clock struck.

A day or two later, when things were to some extent arranged, I invited Jonathan to demonstrate his organ. It is a typical piece of Victorian carved furniture and is driven by pedal power so demands athletic prowess as well as more musical ability than I will ever possess. Dubiously, I wondered what piece of music he would select, thinking at the time that most fourteen-year-olds are only interested in loud pop music. He selected the *Prelude and Fugue* by J. S. Bach, but his father said that he played it too fast.

Les is one of the foremost makers of miniature furniture (that is how we met them originally). He likes to make, in one-twelfth scale, reproductions of eighteenth century furniture, and we possess just a very few of his pieces. Now he has his workroom upstairs on the way to the dolls' houses, and our visitors are intrigued to watch him at work and to talk to him, as he explains that everything he makes has to be in the same manner as the original, scaled down.

Almost all of our house guests have seemed compulsive about bringing pebbles from the beach into the house and creating sculptures by arranging them in piles on the spare bedroom windowsill. This is harmless but they do leave them in place for us to tidy away later. Some of our guests also attempt, usually rather badly, to paint pebbles. The only artist we have met so far who does it really well is Anne Dunford, who paints accurate pictures of the seabirds to be found here which make most attractive paperweights. Jonathan is also a budding artist and good at cartooning. He has invented *Loddles,* strange animals which he claims live only in Lihou rabbit holes. He paints them on stones and also on T-shirts, and anywhere else where it is allowed. Loddles all have large red noses and hairy legs.

Les and Anne, Patricia and myself all take turns at the various jobs which need to be done whilst the Island is open. When either of the Dunford children are here, or indeed any other house guests, everybody helps. All of this makes our tourists feel what they are, callers who are welcomed into a private home.

One of our local visitors said to me that Lihou is full of ghosts and at no price would he stay here for a night. There is a story of a murder which occurred in the time of the monks, but the details are sketchy and it is not a matter of importance. We have lived before in a haunted house (in Malta) and I can only say that the ghosts then were exceptionally friendly, curious about our doings certainly, but charming. If there are any ghosts in Lihou, we have yet to have the pleasure of meeting them.

Not far from the Venus Pool, on the north side of the Island is La Roche de la Fontaine, also known sometimes as La Roque aux Morts, because so it is said (a hundred years or so ago) some drowned sailors were laid out here, prior to burial in a Guernsey churchyard. The story that they were buried here is apparently untrue. La Roche de la Fontaine is a natural outcrop with a protected hollow below it, that fills up rapidly after rain. There are large stones around it, and some people have thought they are an ancient stone circle surrounding the pool, but it is quite a stony part and I do not think this is an early site.

Mostly in Guernsey, and in rural England too, every field has a name. If Lihou fields ever had names, these have fallen into disuse. Apart from the names I have mentioned, the southern peninsula facing L'Erée Head is called Lissroy (pronounced Leroy) and the furthest part of Lihoumel is known to fishermen as Corner Rock, but I have not heard any other popularly accepted names. In fact most of the rocks around the west coast of Guernsey have names, and this is easy to understand since at different states of the tide, each one of them is a menace to fishing boats.

We are often asked if we possess a boat. For a long time the answer

Emptying the Wishing Well.

was no, and we were determined not to own one because we thought that possession would mean that we would be pressed to use it to deliver stranded tourists back to Guernsey, and this might lead to difficulties should we think the weather too bad. Also, a boat may only be used at high water or within two hours of it, because otherwise it would entail a long walk across the rocks to get to the sea, and a boat anchored at low water would be half a mile or so out to sea at high tide. Some of those rocks lie just below the surface at every stage of the tide ready to cut a hole in the bottom of an unsuspecting boat. I certainly would not be prepared to offer a ride back to Guernsey in my boat, or indeed to travel in it myself without an experienced person to help me. Fortunately Les Dunford is both experienced and cautious and I have complete confidence in his ability with it. In fact it spends much of its time except in summer upside down in the garden, but it became a spectacular feature with the name *Lihou Island* showing on its bows in Guernsey's Europa stamps for 1988, when the theme was "transport".

It is a matter for regret, as far as we are concerned, that we have not been successful in gardening here. The garden is fully enclosed with a high wall, but the wind still defeats us, so does the amount of work involved with our visitors. In the past, in Malta and in Guernsey, it has been our pleasure to create ponds and water gardens as well as the more conventional flower gardens. We decided that if we could not have a proper garden, at least we could have a decorative pond. I started, in June 1988, to dig a pond by the kiosk, outside the garden wall. It was August before it was completed and by then Patricia had decided that what I was making looked like a wishing well, and that we would support the Great Ormond Street Wishing Well Appeal. This had already been running since the start of the year. The pond is about three feet deep, with walls of old bricks, plastered on the inside and lined outside in local granite so nobody knows how dubious is my skill as a bricklayer. Hopefully, I filled the pond and was pleasantly surprised to find it hardly leaked at all. The Bailiff, as Patron of the local appeal, kindly agreed to throw in the first coin. I am afraid the ducks think the water is entirely for their benefit, so it needs frequent cleaning.

People are extraordinarily generous. By the time the Bailiff arrived on the second day of the first tide cycle after I had filled it, several visitors had anticipated him and I was able to give him a cheque for more than £9. The money has continued to pour in to the pond, and at the end of 1988 a total of £200 had been given. Usually, when we empty the pond for cleaning we also take the money out, or sometimes Jonathan puts on his wet suit. The money is collected in a collander and put to dry on the cooker before it goes to the bank.

I was approached by a continental film company wanting to make a television feature of the Channel Islands. They asked permission to show a little girl, playing on this Island, then returning to the Causeway to find herself stranded, so sitting down and crying. As the producer pointed out, the child would know that neither she nor her accompanying film crew were really stranded and that they would be rescued by boat. He told me to think of the publicity that I would get as a result. Actually, people come here in large numbers during the summer because the Island attracts them, and we only want extra publicity if it is very good. I told him that people do not get stranded here (at least we take precautions to prevent it) and that I would never allow a child to sit on the beach (or anywhere else) crying. The producer then said that he would like to use Lihou as the background for the same story set on an unidentified rock, but I asked them what publicity we would then have.

We have considered Lihou as a possible venue for shooting film sequences for one of the more respectable television series. These people have to work to a tight schedule which cannot involve waiting for the sun to come out. Therefore enormous arc lights are used, and so far the electricity problem has proved insoluble.

Sometimes people suggest to us that we should exploit the Island more, and some of the ideas offered have struck us as being eccentric. Lihou is quite a powerful place, to be treated with respect, and I would hate to think of it being abused in our ownership. I once reminded someone that the Occupation Forces blasted a hole in Lihou and four years later the Germans were defeated.

CHAPTER SIX
How d'you do and what do you do?

When he was in residence, or when his caretaker was here, the previous owner used to have a stall selling picture postcards and his books, etc. We have replaced this with a small summer house which makes quite a pretty kiosk. Having crossed the Causeway, people like a soft drink, and perhaps some home-made biscuits, and we have our own picture postcards. During the summer people often like to buy kites for the children (there is usually a good wind). On one occasion we sold four within ten minutes, and they looked so pretty being carried back across the Causeway.

Naturally, tourists who come often bring their cameras, and fortunately our shop is now able to supply them with films. We have found that many of our visitors (having rested on the benches) start their walk by photographing the notice which welcomes visitors to Lihou Island (with or without the wife standing near it) and this no doubt begins the section in the album, of photographs of Lihou during a Channel Islands' holiday.

Many people come over here, a little out of puff, and tell us that they consider themselves very fit to have achieved the crossing on foot at the age of 77 or whatever. I have to tell them that the record so far is a lady aged 91 but she did bring her baby sister who was only 89. I think that she had been known as the baby sister for the last 89 years. The gentleman's record is 83 and at the other end of the scale the record is minus some months.

We keep a visitors' book which is situated for convenience in the kiosk, where it is safely out of the way of any passing showers. Quite apart from the fact that people like to leave a record of their visits, it is useful to us because it tells what proportion of our visitors are locals enjoying the fresh air and how many are tourists seeing us for the first time. It also tells us how many are from the U.K., and how many come from the Continent, or further afield. We have had visitors, of course, from Australia and New Zealand, and Canada and U.S.A., but also from Papua New Guinea and from Ethiopia. In our experience, whenever the Germans come we sell out of hard boiled eggs very rapidly, and surprisingly most of the Swiss who visit us are not good at speaking English. I regret that I am hopeless at foreign languages, and we do feel that we should take steps to have informative notices here in German.

In the winter we get far more Guernseymen than tourists, and that is only partly because there are fewer tourists out of season. Many local people regard Lihou as being too popular in the summer and deliberately come only when it is not crowded.

To some extent, being open is for us merely a continuation of what we used to do when we were in Berkshire, because our donkey stud then was open to the public and might attract even more visitors in the summer than we do now. In those days we did not have the certain relief that the tide would come in fairly soon. Recently, by popular request, we have decided to start selling ice cream again. We were reluctant to do this for a long time, because ice cream, like cigarettes, can mean litter. In fact our visitors are thoroughly nice, responsible people (less desirable tourists do not want to make the effort of crossing the Causeway) and we do not have much of a litter problem. We asked the local suppliers, and when the manager came to call on us he told us that he did not need a reference, he had checked up on our record of twenty years and more ago in Berkshire on his computer.

We learn to know in advance the questions which we shall be asked. The first is always when is low tide. It is extraordinary how many people will come here without checking on this first. In fact nobody needs to know what time low tide is, they want to know how long they may stay here in safety, as it may be some time after low water before the tide is again high enough to cover the Causeway. We do nowadays put up a blackboard stating the time, so that everybody can see it, and in the winter when we have few visitors we may usually warn each of them personally and even count them in and out. In the summer this is impossible, but I, or one of my friends goes round about ten minutes before danger time warning people to go. On one occasion, walking round as the tide came in. I heard noises from behind a big rock. I went to investigate and found a couple of holidaymakers, of blond Scandinavian appearance, happy to be alone together. I had to tell them to get their clothes on quick but they did not like being disturbed.

The next question is "Do many people get stranded?" Fortunately, the answer is very few indeed, and now that we know more about how to run this Island, I hope the answer is none at all. We are told that we should ring a bell, or even fire a gun (we do not possess either of these) but we prefer personal contact. If people are nice enough to visit us, we will try to tell them when it is time to go home. In any case bells or other noises would only create turbulence. One lady did tell my wife that high tide was not until nine p.m. and so there was no need to go any earlier than that. Fortunately the lady discovered in time that the Causeway is covered well before half tide, and in fact at high tide there may be as much as thirty feet of water over it.

People want to know how we get our letters and newspapers. Before we moved in, I called on the Post Office, and agreed that it was impossible to expect the postman to swim across daily. In fact we have a locked box (once an electricity sub-station) on the Guernsey side, and tides

permitting, I walk across daily, usually as soon as the Causeway is clear, and on a sunny summer day I have counted myself saying Good Morning ninety-nine times before I reached the other side. One day I was a little bit late and people were already crossing and some had arrived. It was in midsummer, when the Causeway is pleasantly free of seaweed, but on this occasion there was one large piece, well below the tide mark. A lady who did not know who I was picked up this strand and showed it to me. "These people do not keep the place very tidy, do they?" I felt it was best to agree.

We have been asked what all those rocks dotted around the Island are for. Well, I am afraid that I have no answer to that, the whole Island, like Gibraltar, is a rock.

One young lady, hardly yet a teenager, but accompanied by several young men of her own age, wanted to know if she *had* to sign the visitors' book, because she did not want Mummy to know where she had been. In the end she put in her first name, but not her address. This was unfortunate, because she left her bathing towel behind, and we could not post it on to her. Another young couple of schoolchildren were not so modest. They bracketed their names together and wrote 'lovers'.

Lost property is a perennial problem, and it is surprising the things which get handed in. A pair of binoculars, good quality but in a very dirty case, with no owner's name. Two years later we had a telephone call claiming them. I still have in my safe a lady's purse with a £5 note and the return half of a railway ticket, but no clue as to the owner's name.

We are frequently asked what we do for water and for electricity, more occasionally what do we do about drainage (we have our own filter bed). What do we do with our kitchen rubbish? We carry it across the Causeway and leave it every Tuesday for the dustmen, and when the tides are wrong we have to wait until next week. One fussy and rather plump lady asked what we eat when the tides are bad and we cannot cross the Causeway. Actually, we eat mostly out of the deep freeze exactly the same way as we do when we can cross but we assured her that we ate stranded tourists. She looked worried and went home early.

We have many old Guernseymen who come to see us. One of them told me that he was made redundant when the iodine factory closed in 1935 and had not visited since. Another was a man who had been swimming in the Venus Pool as a boy when he had been fetched to get ready for evacuation in 1940. He had never been back to Guernsey until now, when he had come with his daughter, son-in-law and grand-children, all of whom he told to have a swim. The kids said that they did not like sea bathing in November.

The Venus Pool has always been popular. It is a chain of rocks running round the extreme western end of the Island, overlooking Lihoumel, and at high water is completely submerged. As the tide goes out, the rocks appear and a long, narrow pool is left, washed clean by every tide. There is a similar "Venus" pool in Sark, and presumably this one was named after it. One visitor, who might well be described as a fussy Mum told me that her daughter (aged about ten) wished to swim in the Venus Pool. She wanted to know if it was properly chlorinated. I assured her that the water had been changed that morning before she arrived. A scientist to whom I told this story said that I should have told her that chlorine is now out of date and the best pools (such as ours) use iodination.

Some people appear to believe that because this Island is open for them to share in its pleasures, they are at liberty to ask us any sort of personal question that comes into their heads, and even to air their political views.

It is natural for people to ask whether Anne Dunford is our daughter and Les our son-in-law (in fact they are no relation) and whether we have other children (yes, we do, a daughter and two sons, all married and in England) but we are sometimes a little surprised when we are asked how much money we make out of our souvenir shop. In fact the answer is that we do not make a profit, but it does help towards the running expenses of the Island and if the Island is to remain open for your pleasure as well as ours, it should be kept safe and clean and properly insured. The special equipment we require which other people do not such as a fourwheel drive car with trailer and an old builder's dumper (probably the only one in private ownership) is not cheap, to buy or to maintain and everything needs to be either waterproof and salt proof or replaced frequently.

When Patricia is asked whether our occupation is profitable she normally counters by asking her enquirer what he does for a living and whether his salary is sufficient, and very rarely do people have the grace to see that this is the same question in reverse.

Most people take the attitude that they are surprised that we allow them here, let alone welcome them, and ask why we do not keep the place to ourselves. Quite apart from being delighted to see people happily enjoying themselves (and frequently, people arriving here looking cross but going home happy) we would not want to break with tradition, nor would we want to turn people away, and we regret that this is necessary when people very occasionally try bringing their dogs.

At the end of a long tide in the summer when we have had thousands of visitors and life has been exhausting it is pleasant to see the tide covering the Causeway and to be fairly confident that we have not missed any visitors on the round up. Perhaps it is possible to find ten minutes to put our feet up before we start feeding the animals. So many people thank us for keeping it open, for welcoming them and ask whether we do not get exhausted.

We have to organise our private arrangements around the tides, going shopping, ordering supplies of fuel oil and so on, even booking ourselves tickets to England at times to suit the tides but what does not occur to most people is that we have to organise our public lives as well. On an early day of good tides the Island may be open from, say, eleven till one-thirty. That is easy, we have lunch at two after we have checked that nobody is left behind and have closed everything up. Two days later the Causeway can be open from noon till three and that means lunch at half past eleven, and if there is a sudden storm and nobody comes we have eaten early for nothing.

This daily variation is the reason why, in spite of being asked frequently, we have so far not extended ourselves to providing morning coffee or afternoon tea. We know this would be welcome, but the change in daily menu would be one problem, and another would be that you keep us quite busy enough already.

In fact we have about six days every fortnight at the neap tide to ourselves with a virtual guarantee that nobody is going to disturb us. The guarantee is not absolute, very occasionally somebody calls by boat.

One summer we had staying with us a friend named Fiona. She regretted that she had not brought her bathing dress to Lihou and spent days agonising whether it really was as safe as we said it was, to bathe in the nude. Eventually she summoned up all her courage and went in, on a beach out of sight from Guernsey, and told us how lovely it was. Suddenly some boys in wetsuits, teenagers, turned up. Fiona had been swimming under water and she surfaced quite close in towards the beach and rose like Botticelli's Venus. I could not rush to her with a towel, but I did ask the boys (who were more embarrassed that she was) to show me their beautiful little boat and led them away. I asked them if the rather small outboard motor was sufficient in the open sea but they assured me that it was, and took the boat out to prove it.

One other unexpected visitor was a very experienced wet suit fisherman who was caught by an unexpected cross current and beached himself here. He sat outside, not wishing to be a nuisance or an uninvited guest. I went and found him and made him welcome, but he had to stay until the Causeway opened and he could walk home at midnight. We had the most delicious local fish, all very fresh, for supper that evening.

Everybody appears to accept that Patricia stays here the whole time and that she is kept busy with her needlework, but many people have asked her "What does your husband *do*?" and even does he travel to work every day by boat? The question is as perennial as do we like living here (why would we stay if we did not love it?) and what do we do for water and how do we get rid of our sewage. To some enquirers we have answered that I write books and magazine articles.

Shortly before the (U.K.) General Election of 1987 one man marched across the Causeway and announced, when I wished him Good Morning, that I would not be allowed to stay here when Mr Kinnock gets in and takes the Channel Islands into the U.K. net. I did not enquire whether this was a personal message delivered with authority from Mr Kinnock, but I did ask who would run the Island after I had been turned out. "We shall put in a Warden." I asked if it would be a salaried warden and was told that this was so, and I asked if I could apply for the job, but there was no answer. The opportunity for applying for a salary for the job I love has not yet occurred, and thankfully, the Channel Islands are not so far in the U.K. net, nor in the E.E.C. so we are not worried by V.A.T. or milk quotas.

One afternoon I stepped from rock to rock across the Causeway going to collect my letters about half an hour before low water. It was in July the last barely crossable day before the neap tides and there was quite a small crowd of intrepid visitors halfway across, wondering if the paved path would dry out any more, wanting to cross and hoping they would not get their feet too wet (the puddles were still very large). I did not want to disappoint them and I told them all that it was the last day before we closed for a week and to be sure to be back in Guernsey within three quarters of an hour. So often tourists elect to come and see us on the last day of their holiday, possibly after the bathing things have been packed and it is disappointing to be told to go away and come back tomorrow or not to come back for nearly a week, so I always encourage them to come, even risking getting their feet a bit wet, if it is safe to do so.

One woman detached herself from the others and asked what right I had to close it to the public. I felt I had to tell her that she was welcome to try coming if she did not mind getting wet up to here and not even King Canute had succeeded in holding back the tides. As far as we are concerned everybody is welcome, provided they are well behaved (and people are) but on the whole we hope they will refrain from talking politics at us.

This Island has a long history of religious practice and our predecessor used to have occasional ecumenical services here with clergy from various branches of the Christian faith. We have not done anything to encourage services here, for one thing, nowadays there are always tourists here in large numbers, greater numbers than the congregation at a service is likely to be and the tourists (who need not be themselves religious) might find it intrusive and disturbing. We have in fact been asked once by the local Roman Catholic community for the use of the Priory for a service. They did not wish to process in state across the Causeway and it was a simple and very happy occasion. I waited until the end of their service and then entered the Church.

Whilst I was waiting, a lady, obviously taking me for a tourist like herself, stood beside me studying the proceedings then suddenly she tugged on my sleeve and pointed to the Priory. "I reckon that's a ruined church." I was delighted to agree, even if this did appear to be a glimpse of the obvious. Another, younger lady with two small children stood listening, her eyebrows going higher and higher. Suddenly the entire congregation crossed themselves and she knew she was in the company of people like herself. She made the sign of the cross, pushed the two children through a hole in the Priory wall and then dived in after them head first, in a most surprisingly athletic manner. She joined in their service with enthusiasm.

I was able to tell them that it so happened that it was the hundred and fiftieth anniversary of the finding of the bronze crucifix by the archaeologist F. C. Lukis in the Priory Church where they were standing, and to tell them how Mrs Cole (curator of the Guernsey Museum) had taken the original to London to the British Museum where a mould had been taken. The crucifix had only recently been returned to the museum but we (and the museum) had just received reproductions of it for sale, and it was our pleasure to present copies to the two priests who came. As invited through their priests, several of the congregation had brought their bathing things and I was pleased that the sun came out and they were able to enjoy the Venus Pool.

Amongst those present was Mrs Piriou and it was then that I first met her. Subsequently she came back to see us again with her brother Tom Babbé and they gave me the details of the history of the iodine factory which appear in chapter two.

CHAPTER SEVEN
Living With The Tides

Yachtsmen should know all about tides, most people know of their existence, having learnt about them at school and then forgotten. To us, tides are so important that they control our lives. The Channel Islands have some of the biggest in the world. Tides are ruled principally by the moon, and broadly when we have a full moon or a new moon the Causeway is crossable. This is called a spring tide (nothing to do with spring and autumn). At half moon we have the opposite, a neap tide and for more than a third of the days in the year the Causeway does not uncover at all.

It is not quite as easy as that (nothing is) for the biggest tides happen a day or two *after* the full or new moon and the smallest tides a day or two *after* the half moon. The sun also has an effect, but this is the reverse, at the *equinox* (23rd March and 23rd September) the tides are enhanced and at midsummer's day and midwinter day (the *solstices*) they are reduced. If a full moon coincides with the equinox the tides can be sensational. High water occurs roughly every twelve and a half hours, but even this varies from day to day. Anyway, the tides are about an hour later each day.

All this may be predicted, and local tide tables are available in most harbour towns. When high tide is exceptionally high, low tide is exceptionally low. The tides are also affected by the barometer, but here the effect is different. If the barometer is high, the air pressure pushes the sea away, and both high and low tides are lower than expected, the barometer in fact making a very considerable difference. The tides are also affected by the wind, but that is a complete lottery, one wind may push the sea out, another may hold it up, and the wind can change at any time.

As most people know, Easter happens on the first Sunday after a particular full moon. We may be closed or open for other public holidays, but we do expect a rush always at Easter time. Often it rains and everybody is disappointed.

We use our computer to work out special tide tables for Lihou Island, and these are sent to Radio Guernsey, Channel Television ('Oracle', page 239) various publications circulating in the Channel Islands, and the Tourist Board.

Also anyone may ring us up to ask. We have a radio link telephone, with its aerial pointed at the B.B.C. tower at Pleinmont. It has two frequencies, one to talk and one to listen, so nobody who rings us need realise that it is anything other than a perfectly normal telephone.

We cannot forecast the barometric pressure or the wind, we try to take every thing else into account, even allowing a little for the probability that the pressure will be lower in winter than in summer. On the whole we get it more or less right, but we do try to err very slightly on the side of safety. We can get caught out and may be completely wrong. One Christmas Radio Guernsey said (with our approval) that the Causeway would be open on Christmas afternoon for an hour or more and that we should be delighted if anybody came to wish us the compliments of the season. At least twenty people did come, and were unable to understand when they half crossed the Causeway and found further progress barred by quite a lot of sea. I telephoned Radio Guernsey (and spoke on the air) to say that I was sorry for the barometer, and quite simply, I had got it wrong. Never mind, that evening plenty of people came to L'Erée Head car park and flashed their lights at us as suggested by the radio, and one lady rang up to say that it was a lovely idea to wish us a happy Christmas with flashing headlights only unfortunately she had no car.

We base our own predictions on being able to cross when low water is forecast at a height of 2.80 metres or less, when the Causeway dries out sufficiently with an average barometer to be able to cross wearing good shoes but not necessarily gumboots. It is fortunate for us that low water at this height occurs around the middle of the day, and low water on a neap tide (when the Causeway never uncovers at all) is at socially undesirable times. The Causeway may be open as late as six or seven in the evening, but in winter we always try to get our visitors away before dusk, as crossing the Causeway if you do not know it can be very dangerous in the dark, particularly if the sea is not dead calm.

We are very firm in saying that visitors are not welcome (except by previous arrangement) to come over on an early tide and spend the whole day here, and we never allow camping. This Island is our home and visitors are welcome when the Causeway is open, but we do like to have it to ourselves for part of the day, and all the night. If we ever allowed friends, or anybody to camp, the tent would be seen and we would be inundated with requests from others who would very reasonably say "Why not me, too?"

People seem to be fascinated by the risk of being caught by the tide and stranded, and it is one of the first questions visitors ask. I have no doubt that before we lived here it must have been a not infrequent occurence and I have heard recently of a mother who was frantic when her young son was compelled to spend a night sheltering in the Priory ruins with no extra clothing and no way of letting anybody know what had happened. He was rescued early next morning. Through the years, as I have mentioned, various fictional stories (and verses) have been written

Visitors arriving.

concerning Lihou, and many appear to depend for their plots on stranding, possibly because nothing else exciting happens or comes to the imagination.

In our first year here, we watched one afternoon as a pretty yacht in full sail went through the Braye de Lihou (where the Causeway is when the tide is out). This is in fact perfectly safe if one knows the local waters, and the secret is to keep well over to the Lihou side where the water is deeper. The owner did not know this, but he was fortunate. He was in fact on his first trip outside home waters in his new yacht. He sailed on down towards Pleinmont, then decided that he had found the most beautiful place and came back to anchor for the night. I tried to shout to him, to tell him that he was in danger, but my voice was not sufficient and waving my arms only resulted in a friendly wave back. As the tide went out the yacht started to bump, and he spoke to the Harbourmaster on his radio. The Harbourmaster sent out the St John's Ambulance rubber dinghy (which has a very powerful outboard engine) and that pulled the yacht off. I heard later that the only damage was scratches to the paint. We could not ourselves talk to the harbourmaster or do anything else to help as it was before we had our telephone.

Very occasionally we get people here who are apparently complete idiots. One day when the tide did not clear the Causeway, but the line of rocks was visible we saw a schoolmaster with eighteen subteenagers in bathing things wading across. They were all wet well above the knees, but one little girl had toppled over. I went out to meet them and quickly checked that they were from the Mainland. I am afraid that I was very rude to the schoolmaster in front of the kids and told him that he was putting their lives at risk. I got him to admit that he had read the notice on the Guernsey side which specifically states "If any part of the Causeway is awash do not attempt the crossing." One of the boys said "I told you it was dangerous — sir." They all waded back. Later a friend of ours telephoned, furious, to say that he had been in the car park, that he had walked down to the notice with the schoolmaster and had read the notice to him. He had offered to lead them to safe beaches. Our friend then telephoned the local paper, and we were featured next day.

This led to considerable discussion in the Parish Meeting. The local dignitaries decided that Lihou is an important tourist attraction, that it is right to encourage people when it is safe, and necessary to prevent them coming when it is not. Nobody in Guernsey (at least not that part of Guernsey) was prepared to be responsible for putting up a notice forbidding access and taking it down again. Therefore they decided that I should be responsible for coming across the Causeway when it is dangerous to put up a notice saying it is dangerous. I said that if I put up a notice forbidding access I would not be able to get home without disobeying it (always assuming that I made it on the outward trip), so they thought again. They said that they would put up a notice saying that nobody could cross when I was flying a red flag. This posed lots of difficulties. For one thing, it implied that if no flag was flying, it was safe. What if there was a storm, and the flag was blown away? I said very firmly that the Red Flag was not my politics, and the subject was dropped.

CHAPTER EIGHT
Past, Present and Future

I thought it remarkable that in 1983 three Channel Islands should have been for sale at once. There are in fact only four with houses on them which are not in multiple ownership, and Lihou Island was the last of the three to come on the market. Herm has not been on the market since 1945 and Major Wood and his family are very happy there. Not for a minute did we consider buying one of the other two. Every island has an individual flavour, and neither of them was for us.

We were living in a beautiful little house in St Martin's but we did find it very small. We thought of moving and looked very seriously at Sark, which certainly has claims to be special and indeed unique. Sark, like everywhere else, has its disadvantages, and Sarkese people say that these contribute to its charm. Sark is inaccessible, to go there from England involves flying to Guernsey and taking a taxi to the harbour, or going on a lengthy ferry trip. Either way there may be quite a long wait (sometimes even overnight) before catching the Sark ferry. It is famous as the island which does not allow motor cars, and therefore its roads are unmetalled, but every *tenement* holder is allowed a tractor, so very sensibly they use these as if they were cars and also earn money using them as delivery vehicles. You cannot readily take a tractor from Sark to Guernsey, and you certainly may not use it there as a car. It would be better, to my mind, to allow very small cars in Sark, but no Sarkese would agree, nor I think would the tourists who delight in doing it the hard way, travelling to an hotel on a trailer behind a tractor or going round the Island on a hired bicycle and feeling stiff for a week afterwards. It is true, incidently, that even if one has not ridden a bicycle for forty years one may still start again without any difficulty.

Another of Sark's distinctions is that no aeroplanes are allowed to land there or even to cross, but an exception was made when H.M. the Queen Mother visited by helicopter.

Sark is small, all the fields are small and so are the houses, at least those we have seen. The choice is limited. If our house in Guernsey was for us cramped, we doubted if we could improve on it by going to Sark.

Mr Leonard Matchan bought Brecqhou more than twenty years ago and it was freehold. A strange man, who boasted of his socialism and claimed to despise everything that he himself stood for, because he was proud of being a successful businessman who made a very great deal of money in his long career. If Sark is inaccessible, Brecqhou is more so, even from Sark which is only yards away (although the intervening channel is deep), unless like Mr Matchan you are rich enough to own a private helicopter and to employ a full time pilot for it. When he bought Brecqhou he paid a fair price (by 1960s standards) for such a remote island, freehold. He offered it for sale on lease, subject to various restrictive covenants, at an asking price of four million. Although the price was later reduced by a quarter, he never did find anybody interested.

Jethou is a completely different proposition. It is a direct Crown lease which at the time of sale had only another twenty-two years to run, but an extension was negotiable with the Crown. It has cottages (and tenants, the staff of the late owner) and a house of quality. To many people its great attraction would be that it is a private estate where nobody may go without invitation. The owner needs to be a yachtsman, or to have a boatman on his staff. I am sure that the existing staff are excellent, and indeed the late Sir Charles Hayward who used to own it would have required the best, but this means a substantial wage roll, and in any case, even had we wanted it, the asking price was way out of our reach. Jethou took quite a time before finding the right owners for itself.

Herm is the perfect public park, and tourists love strolling in it, and do so by the boat load during the season when the weather is fair and the sea calm. Herm did not suffer as a target during the war, its field walls are intact and it boasts the largest herd of pedigree Guernsey cattle in the Channel Islands (strange that this should be in an offshore island). Because it has been farmed for so long and so well, it is comparatively weed free, with no thistles and bracken.

Lihou has a different flavour. More rocky, wilder and windswept without any prospect of being able to grow trees. When we came here, people were worried because we said we intended to tidy it up. This did not mean that we were going to spray artificial fertiliser everywhere or mow down the bracken, which is a very good cover for nesting birds. The island is interesting because there are few enough places in the British Isles today where one can be certain that no spraying has ever taken place, either deliberately or by drifting from the neighbour's fields.

We have tidied the Island and we continue to do so. There is now no barbed wire, and gradually we are removing the fallen masonry from the field walls. Periodically we have a massive weeding operation in the Priory and we have a battle every year against ragwort and hogweed. It is hardly necessary to say that we spend much time removing litter, but although we do get the occasional cigarette end from our visitors, on the whole they are very good and attentive to our requests not to leave litter. Most of it is washed up from the sea, some of it I regret, deposited in the sea from other islands, and some from ships. We receive frequently, plastic bottles which formerly contained detergent and are marked "Property of the Ministry of Defence, not to be used on H.M. submarines" which says something for the standards of the Royal Navy today.

It is strange how one gets into the habit of sorting one's own domestic litter automatically. People living in towns (as most people do nowadays) cannot have bonfires, even if they own a small garden. We have one almost every day when the wind is not too strong, and we have just rebuilt the incinerator on the site where apparently it has always been. For us, refuse means dogmeat tins and such like to be taken across once a week when the tide obliges. Any paper, and the inevitable cardboard cartons, go in the incinerator.

Apart from living by the tides there are certain skills which need to be developed and certain tasks which have to be done regularly or disaster strikes. Once a fortnight I have to top up the chlorinator in the loft. This looks a venerable machine, in its mahogany case, but surprisingly it is quite modern and highly efficient, but the case is only mahogany faced ply. Before we obtained a licence for a self catering flat the hotels' inspector came to see us and for safety considered that the water inspector should also come. This latter gentleman examined our chlorinator and said that it must be replaced with a more modern arrangement. He tested the water and found it was absolutely spot on.

We did try in 1987 letting the cottage at the back as self catering holiday accommodation and our tenants, mainly honeymooners, thoroughly enjoyed themselves. We enjoyed having them but we found that it was only attractive in the summer and at precisely the time when we were at our busiest. We decided reluctantly that it was extra work just when we could not tackle it. Guernsey's tourist trade is flourishing and there is some shortage of accommodation so we regretted having to be uphelpful but I am sure it was the correct decision. Incidentally, Guernseymen are themselves sober and honest and the tourist trade attracts similar people. Perhaps I am being unfair in saying that only pleasant people want to make the effort to come across the Causeway, the truth may be that there are normally only pleasant people on either side.

The first of the month is the day when we test the batteries, and there seems to be an endless number of them, consuming large quantities of distilled water. A battery on each of our two big generators (we also have a small portable generator for emergency use, started by hand). Heavy duty batteries for the invertor which gives us light when the generator is off and batteries for the telephone, to say nothing of the motor car and the dumper. Once, when I was doing the batteries I finished a bottle of distilled water and grabbed the next one off the shelf. It was only later that I discovered the ghastly truth. An electrician's apprentice working here some months previously had left a half consumed bottle of clear lemonade amongst the water bottles. I breathed in quite an amount of the gas which the battery produced and realised how the soldiers must have felt when they were wounded with poison gas. We had to buy a new battery from the Mainland and knowing how expensive are these heavy duty ones (used by fork lift trucks and the like), we were thankful I had only wrecked one.

The other fairly frequent task is to clean the cooker. We have an oil fired Rayburn and its burner gets caked periodically with soot. It has to be turned off and left to cool, then stripped down (rubber gloves). Preferably this is a task to be done on a warm morning, as it will be quite a time before it is hot enough again and heating the bath water.

We were rung up by a lady who announced "I'm a breaker, and I would like to come and spend the night in Lihou with my friends." Further conversation revealed that "breakers" is the technical term for radio fanatics, somewhere between hams and people who have a C.B. radio in the car. The cottage at the back of the house was vacant at the time and we invited them to stay with us, after they had come for a preliminary reconnaissance. There were several of them, of whom the youngest, the head breaker's son, was then aged twelve. He was much intrigued with a wood burning stove we had just installed, and he wanted to know if he could get it hot enough to boil a kettle. He could, and did, but the room was unbearably hot for those breakers who were to sleep in it, and afterwards we were a bit short of firewood.

The breakers had a theory that there was nothing between Lihou and America and so if they tried at night they might get a reply (in the early evening by local time) from New York. In the event the weather was filthy and although they erected an enormous aerial they only penetrated three miles to the west, to Les Hanois lighthouse where the keeper said that it was quite a change to receive radio messages instead of smoke signals from Lihou.

Les Hanois is on an outlying rock, the furthest part of the chain which surrounds the west coast of Guernsey and makes navigation inshore impossible except to the smallest boats. At present it is one of the few remaining British lighthouses to be manually operated. Its importance has declined now that the shipping lanes have been rearranged further from the coast of Guernsey, but we do still see the occasional ship on the horizon. Robbie, one of the keepers is a well known local character, and when he is on duty there he often puts a message in a bottle and lets it drift to sea. We have had Christmas greetings from him by this method, and a mutual friend has threatened to send the next message off to Switzerland to be returned to Robbie with a Lake Geneva postmark.

Guernseymen have a tremendous and perhaps slightly sentimental love for their offshore islands. They are torn between feeling how wonderful it would be to live in one, and being thankful that their homes are where they are, with a supermarket in reach and everything available. Tradespeople know our difficulties and appreciate that we need deliveries at a specific time to catch the tide. Many of them indeed pride themselves on keeping a copy of the tide table by the telephone so that they may tell us when we ring on which day they may come, before we can tell them.

We have frequent discussions about what we could do, and should do for the future. In general we are well satisfied with the Island as it is and we have no great plans for change or expansion. Guernsey's Tourist Board recognises that we constitute one of the attractions of the Bailiwick. The newspapers sometimes get on to us, trying to create or anticipate news where none exists so far, and even write about us without appearing to know (or perhaps to care) where to find Lihou Island.

For a long time I wanted a trademark, or as it is now called, a logo, and this became an urgent question when we decided that our kiosk should sell T-shirts and sweat-shirts. Our first four-wheel drive car had the name painted on the spare wheel cover but I was not very happy about the style of the lettering although it was clear enough. One day when we were in London I sat our son-in-law down at the dining table and told him to design a logo. This he did in less than ten minutes and it has since appeared on car stickers (much appreciated as a talking point because it is quite a challenge to ask where Lihou Island is) and on many different souvenirs. Fortunately we have a good copying machine and can even reproduce it on notepaper which looks very smart. We do also have it signwritten on the spare wheel cover, which we find also does duty as an eye catcher at the back of the stand when Patricia sometimes takes her miniature carpets to craft fairs.

The Island is expansive, it is able and willing to accept any number of visitors at once, at least we have never found it overcrowded but the accommodation in the house is limited and we have constant difficulty in finding storage space. Occasionally in the summer we have to restrict the numbers coming to see the dolls' houses because there are sufficient people inside already, but everybody who wishes gets to see them before it is time to go back to Guernsey.

I have in my office a file called *"Letters of Appreciation"*. It is a very thick file but it does contain three letters of complaint, including one from a lady who wrote to say that although we do not allow dogs the geese made up for it and she had got her shoes grubby. (We did have rather a lot of geese at the time, and we were quite pleased when somebody wanted some to graze a field). I wondered what the French lady who tripped across the Causeway in high heeled patent leather fashion boots thought about the going underfoot. Sensibly, that lady took things as she found them. Many of our visitors stop to thank us and to tell us that they have enjoyed the Island, the animals, and the dolls' houses, and we appear to get more and more happy visitors each year, so it seems that we have got our act together more or less right. I hope so.

CHAPTER NINE
The Dolls Houses

Patricia has always been keen on sewing and very good at the finest work. When we moved from England to Malta we bought a Victorian dolls house because she wanted something to occupy her mind now that we no longer had our business. She thought it would be fun to furnish it and we could bring miniature things back with us when travelling by air. From this grew a collection and she now has about twenty. Naturally they are carpeted in fine needlework, and we have made up stories about the people who live in them. We were asked, when we were living in Guernsey to open them to the public because our neighbours were holding a garden fete for charity. This was so successful that other people asked us for private visits.

Subsequently, when we moved here, and got ourselves and our home a bit organised, we opened the dolls house exhibition for an Easter weekend. It proved so popular, particularly amongst boarding house keepers and owners of small hotels (who wanted something to recommend to their guests) that we opened the exhibition on a permanent basis. This entails one of us being in the house the whole time that the Causeway is open, and quite a lot of extra work when it is not, so we make a small admission charge, but only for indoor exhibitions. Lihou has always been open to the public, and we like to see people enjoying themselves. As far as we are concerned it always will be, and there will never be any charge to visitors who want to walk round and enjoy it. Because we do not issue admission tickets we have no way of telling accurately how many people come.

Our first, large Victorian house had no furniture when we bought it, but the original wall paper was intact. Generally, it was dirty, and the staircase was in a state of collapse. It looked very like a real house which has been empty and unloved for a long period. We set about spring cleaning and restoring it, and on our occasional visits to England bought miniature furniture and made other bits ourselves.

We needed a picture for the dining room. A colour photograph of a family picture looked perfect, framed in small pieces of wood. As far as possible we used ordinary everyday objects disguised and converted into miniature furniture. Patricia started to make bedding and carpets, but our first house is still carpeted with those miniature mats which are

sold in carpet shops to put under the telephone or for use on tables. They happened to fit exactly and are in period, but a little too thick.

We had a piece of good fortune, one of our friends knew someone who made dolls as a hobby. This gave us an opportunity to make up a story about the people who live in the house. The first figure was a very old and sick lady, who lies in bed, attended by the doctor (with a correct period stethoscope) and a nurse. In the drawing room, and looking remarkably unconcerned, are her son and daughter-in-law, obviously waiting to inherit. Nanny is around, trying to keep the children quiet. The son is playing with his diavolo (a wonderful period toy) but he has his train set laid out on the floor just outside the sickroom where it looks inevitable that the nurse will tread on it and go flying. Only the elder daughter, in the drawing room with her parents is well behaved. She is mopping up after the puppy. As Nanny holds the baby, I thought at one time of taking her apron off, turning her into the eldest daughter, and making her stand pathetically outside the front door as Father consigns her to Outer Darkness. This is in any case impractical today, as all the houses have their fronts off so that visitors may look into them. The kitchen was a great deal of fun, and it was not easy to keep it in period, now it has Cook, and the Gardener with a splendid bunch of carrots and a visitor in the chair, obviously discussing the inevitable changes which are coming. I wanted to have a policeman with whiskers holding his top hat in one hand and an enormous mug of tea in the other, but the doll maker was no more. The sitting room has a mirror above the fireplace, and people usually do not succeed in photographing it without incorporating the photographer's own portrait there, which spoils the illusion. One of our visitors, who comes here frequently told me with a smile that in her opinion Granma was looking better and that very soon she would recover and send her grasping family packing, making a new will in favour of the cats home. This is a contingency we had not previously considered.

Now, with all the dolls houses (there are more than twenty) on public exhibition, each of them has a descriptive story on a card. This has brought home to people that a dolls house must have a theme, and that it is a remarkable exercise for the imagination to change the scale of life when the stories are so believable. Many people have come, wondering if the exhibition is merely old toys, and been surprised to find that dolls houses are definitely not for kids (although we do have one small dolls house on the floor for play, so children are not forgotten). Lots of people have told us that the old dolls house is still up in the loft, but that now it will come down and be rearranged, with a family to live in it. Generally, these are "Triang" dolls houses which were sold remarkably cheaply, even by the standards of the times, in toy shops before and after the war, until unfortunately Lines Brothers went out of business.

The story for the Victorian house is in fact the longest of any, but our visitors find time to enjoy them all. It used to start by stating that the house dates from 1860, but Vivienne Greene, the greatest expert on antique dolls houses, who has a regular annual holiday in Guernsey and always comes to see us, stated that it should be dated 1870, so the story had to be retyped. Another (the doctor's house, which I shall mention later) we had as being Edwardian, but she said 1860. Mrs Greene has her own museum, in a charming purpose-made building, the Rotunda, near Oxford.

We were given another antique dolls house by some people who came to stay with us in Malta. This is much smaller, only two rooms. It is fascinating, because it is French, and covered inside and out with lithographed paper, still in good condition. Patricia decided to furnish it as far as possible in the French taste of its period, — La Belle Epoch. The first object to go in it was a miniature photograph of my grandfather which had been given to us by the French lady in whose arms he died. He was a very lovely, and loving man and was aged 91 at the time, in 1936, so she had also reached a great age by the time we met her on our honeymoon. When she died in 1966 she was 99, and still lived with her maid who had been with her most of their lives. This photograph gave us the theme for the house. Today it is very fussily furnished, and has a rather blousy doll in residence with her poodle and a gentleman who has come to call. It proved to be quite an intellectual exercise to write the appropriate story for this one in a manner which could be appreciated by children without offending their parents. We took it to a crafts fair in Guernsey one year, and it gave us much amusement to see how many of the visitors read the story about it and passed on without a smile.

By the time we left Malta around Christmas 1981 we had five or six dolls houses, mostly bought locally, although we did have a moment of embarrassment when we advertised in the local paper to see if we could acquire more and found that "Dolls House" in Maltese is a colloquiallism which means something completely different.

Fortunately, we have one large room upstairs, formerly a loft which we converted and redecorated for all the dolls houses. They have overflowed, some on the landing and one in the hall, but the exhibition is still nicely compact.

One of our problems at present is that people wanting ice cream have to come into the front hall of the house, where we keep the freezer, and get muddled with the people coming in to see the dolls houses. Also, soft drinks and home made biscuits and sweets are for sale at the kiosk (no doubt people who have just walked all of half a mile across the Causeway feel in need of them to increase their blood sugar), and that is not close to the ice cream sales. This is something which we hope to correct.

The first house that visitors see is at the bottom of the stairs, rather confusingly called The Green House, because that is its colour, it is not a conservatory. It is just a modern house, a fine example of modern commercial craftsmanship, but not in itself exceptional.

This house defied us for ages, because it did not offer a theme for a story and it had a modern kitchen, a television and a record player, but a parlourmaid from an earlier age. We are now rearranging it as a wedding, with the Bride being dressed by the dressmaker whilst Mother does a hurried tidy up downstairs, the Bride having unwrapped her late presents but not put away the wrapping paper, all the presents (and of course the Champagne) are laid out. In another room the bridesmaids are dressing. The butler is not yet ready, nor is the father of the Bride, but I hope we shall be able to show that the butler has anticipated the celebration and his employer will be suitably cross. Unfortunately, as the wedding itself is still to come we cannot meet the bridegroom, nor know whether the best man still has the ring safely.

We have a very fine "room box" by that great Yorkshire craftsman, Mr Alan Borwell. This is reserved for our best pieces. In it we have put our finest furniture, including several pieces by Les Dunford, some of which we bought several years ago. There is a Pembroke table in mahogany, with inlaid top and legs, a perfect reproduction of an eighteenth century table. Such tables were made with dovetailed joints,

73

and it has its drawer open to show that even this detail has been reproduced in miniature. On it there is an ivory box which contains a complete set of dominoes. Fortunately, Les has a friend, a piano manufacturer and he was able to acquire very small offcuts of ivory from him. There are also examples of work by other well know craftsmen miniaturists.

We had a great deal of fun when we lived in Malta with a house which we called Dove Villa, because we put white doves on its roof. It is a crudely made house dating from perhaps 1910, but probably sold commercially. We made it into a music school and the joke was that the teacher was a doll who much resembled one of the best known and best loved music teachers there. The grand piano is still upstairs, and the lesson continues but some of the children may not be very talented and the fathers have retreated downstairs for a drink.

Over the years we have bought various houses in kit form, partly because they are both cheaper and easier to bring home, and partly because it provides fun in the winter evenings making them up and criticising the designers, who never seem to appreciate that if the front of a house is to open, very strong hinges must be supplied. We have made a conservatory, where the Edwardian lady of the house is trying to cope with her children and her inebriated gardener, all without getting her hands dirty. We also made a grocers shop and found that our young grandson had an unexpected talent for making realistic cheeses and other groceries out of modelling clay and had a natural sense of scale. Les Dunford made us a bakers shop out of scraps of plywood, all in half a rainy afternoon. It is the shop of Mr Henry Crumb, who is noted for his bread and cakes but not for his hygiene. We have completed, but not yet furnished, a fine corner shop with accommodation over, the type of shop which is featured in the television series *Open All Hours*. In order further to encourage potential miniature enthusiasts we are planning to have a few kits for sale, but naturally we shall have the completed models on display, to prove that it is possible.

Our more recent acquisitions include a house which we bought when we were ourselves exhibiting at the Kensington Dolls House Festival. We thought it was made early in this century but apparently it is mid Victorian. It is a very typical Victorian or Edwardian home, it could be a seaside villa, but this one is going to be, eventually, a doctor's surgery. This gives us, through the winter months, a certain amount of fun. We have been to the Wellcome Museum to see what a surgery of the period had, and we still need to make such things as a sight testing card. Obviously, the letters will spell out a message (we have not decided on it yet) but we shall be quietly amused to see how many of our visitors notice this. We have already the doctor, and his desk and one patient for the waiting room, a small boy with a saucepan stuck over his head.

Our old friend Barry Pope made a house for us. He is a farmer, but his hobby has always been fine woodwork and he has made several houses. This one is modern in style but rather pretentious and so has an upwardly mobile family in it. The twins are having a birthday party which has gone disastrously wrong, the boss's small daughter has fallen downstairs and so on. Father is quite young but ambitious and self important and his bowler hat and brolly are in the hall. Mother has retreated to the bedroom for a quick Vallium and found the cats and kittens scrabbling on the new bedspread, which (as I point out in the story card) has been sewn by Patricia. Meanwhile, Grandfather is alone in the sitting room convinced that it was a dreadful mistake to come for the weekend.

Next door is a very modern house, built from a pattern published by Readers Digest, which was made for his daughter by a Royal Marines sergeant in Malta. When the time came for him to go back to England he sold it to us. In it there is a prosperous family where father is a successful and well qualified technician. He is not ambitious and the people next door do not allow their children to speak to his, but he does own a four poster bed (made out of biros) which they do not.

Whenever he can, Les Dunford sits in his workroom next to the dolls house room during the hours when the Causeway is open, and is pleased to receive visitors and show off his miniature furniture as work in progress. How he can cope with the public, even inviting them in is difficult to understand but he has a smile for everybody, and many a do-it-yourself carpenter has been fascinated to find miniature mahogany furniture is made with miniature tools such as very small circular saws but with the same techniques and skill as full size pieces.

One of our visitors suggested to me that I should provide trestle tables down the centre of the dolls house room so that the houses could be rearranged in the manner of a street. I had to say that this was a suggestion too awful to contemplate. If I provided any more space Patricia would go out at once and buy more dolls houses, but in any case space has to be available to allow visitors to circulate freely.

One lady, having walked round the exhibition told me that the previous week she had been to Windsor Castle and seen Queen Mary's dolls house. She said it was such a pity that the Queen only owned one dolls house, (which lacks a story about the people who live in it) and that our exhibition was much better. I promised not to tell Her Majesty.

Appendix A THE BOTANY OF LIHOU ISLAND by Patience Ryan

Appendix B THE BIRDS OF LIHOU ISLAND by Robert Lihou

Both these appendices originally appeared in *A Brief Guide to Lihou Island* and are reprinted with thanks to their authors.

Appendix A

THE BOTANY OF LIHOU ISLAND
by Patience Ryan

A casual visitor to Lihou might well be forgiven for thinking it is just a small, rocky, somewhat barren windswept island, cut off from Guernsey except for a few days of spring tides.

A closer look would reveal a peaceful and charming Isle, with a surprising number of quite different habitats, each in its own small way providing conditions for a variety of plants.

A small pond nestles in the hollow of a shingle bank, in its muddy surrounds a number of saltmarsh plants grow, as, although the water is fresh seaspray adds salt to the area. Here can be found, each in its season, *Saltmarsh Rush, Prostrate Glasswort, Common Seablite* and *Sea Milkwort*.

On the shingle bank among other plants growing there are *Bittersweet, Sea pinks, Sea Stork's Bill, Sea Beet* (which is a delicious substitute for spinach), *Yellow Horned poppy, Scurvy-grass, Scarlet Pimpernel* and for one brief season *Sea Pea* was noted, a plant not found before in the Channel Islands. It was probably eaten by some of the seaweed eating sheep imported by the previous tenant. It might be worth mentioning that these small sheep ate most of the vegetation in the Island as part of their diet, and kept it closely cropped, but the year after their departure there was a wonderful display of wild flowers.

Some *Tamarisk* trees grow in the shelter of a wall surrounding the house and outbuildings, the only trees in the Island and ideal for seaside conditions with their feathery green leaves and sprays of pink flowers in the summer.

Through the gate on the south side a path leads to the ruins of the Priory. On the slope can be found *Musk Stork's Bill, Lady's Bedstraw, Common Bird's Foot Trefoil, Sea Campion*, with *Sea Spleenwort* on the Priory walls. *Wild Teasel* is sometimes seen here. *English Stonecrop* creeps over some stony outcrops and *Autumn Squill, Lesser Bird's Foot Trefoil, Yellow Bartsia, Fiddle Dock* and *Mossy Pearlwort* are found among grass on the gently sloping ground leading to the spine of the Island.

Atlantic clover, with opaque leaves the first clover to flower may crop up along any of the paths and short turf.

On the extreme west end the soil is thin among the lichen covered rocks. *Sea pinks* and *Buck's Horn Plantain* are the dominant plants here.

On the north facing slopes *Carrot* may be seen with *Lanceolate Plantain, Tormentil,* a small amount of *Ling,* and *Bell Heather, Celandines* growing among grasses of which a number are scattered over the Island, among them, *Cock's Foot, Yorkshire Fog, Red Fescue.*

But the earliest grasses are *Sweet Vernal grass, Small Hair Grass, Silver Hair Grass* and *Early Meadowgrass.*

The north end is another area with shallow soil, with *Buck's Horn Plantain, Sea Pinks* and *Rock Samphire* among the rocks, the leaves of which can be pickled.

But suddenly a change in the vegetation is noted, and on either side of the path leading back to the buildings are *Bracken, Gorse, Bluebells, Common Dog Violets, Wall Pennywort* nestling among cracks in the rocks and *Common Vetch* all flowering at their special times during the year.

Lissroy is mainly covered with rough grass and *Sandsedge* apart from a small area of short turf at the base of large rocks, here *Sea Pinks* make patches of bright colour in the spring.

Many other plants are found scattered about the Island, these include *Chickweed, Docks, Thistles, Spurreys,* members of the *Goosefoot* family, *Clovers, Nettles, Charlock, Common Ceutaury* and *four-leaved All-seed.*

Botanists started taking an interest in the flowers of Lihou about the beginning of the last century, some of the flowers they noted are no longer to be found, but others are new, and at present 120 plants can be seen. Although spring and early summer are the best times of the year to see most of these plants in flower, at almost any other season there will be something of interest to anyone who is fond of nature and wild flowers in particular.

It is interesting to note the analysis of our honey, which shows what flowers our bees were able to find and use:—

1. *Lotus* (Birdsfoot Trefoil)
2. *Trifolium Repens* (White Clover)
3. *Compositae* (Chicory or Dandelion)
4. *Endymion* or other *liliaceae*
5. *Rumex* (Dock)
6. *Umbelliferae* (Hogweed and Cow Parsley)
7. *Acer* (Sycamore/Maple)
8. *Rubus*
9. *Phlox*
10. *Campanula*

Appendix B

THE BIRDS OF LIHOU ISLAND
by Robert Lihou

As Lihou is the most westerly part of the Channel Isles it can be seen from an ornithological point of view as one of the first landfalls for migrant birds. However, due to the lack of high vegetation, feeding and resting opportunities for most passerine species is limited at present to areas of bracken on the north-eastern side of the Island and up on Lissroy. Cover is provided as well in the garden of the house including the tamarisk trees by the boundary walls.

Regularly seen feeding in this vegetation are such migrants as *Chiff-chaffs* and *Willow Warblers,* various other species of warblers and, particularly in the autumn, *Pied Flycatchers* can be seen flying from the tamarisk.

Since the removal of the North Ronaldshay Sheep, the scrub vegetation is beginning to recover and now healthy young growths of brambles are to be found springing up in various parts of the Island, these will in time be considered as a valued source of food and shelter for migrant birds. Early March provides the first indications of the spring migration when *Wheatears* stop and refuel on their journey northwards, white rumps flashing about as they fly from stone to stone in search of tasty grubs to be found in plenty on the grassy slopes and shores of Lihou. It is not unusual to see the larger and brighter subspecies of *Greenland Wheatear* stopping off on spring or autumn passage (wheatears have been known to breed in Guernsey, it is not impossible for this to happen in Lihou).

A good place to look for other members of the Chat family are the walls running along the 'spine' of the Island, here migrant *Whinchats* and *Redstarts* are likely to be seen. Another close relative, the *Black Redstart* is an occasional winter visitor and migrant.

Another March arrival is the *Common Sandpiper,* a wader which is more likely to be heard before it is seen in amongst the rocks on all coasts. *Grey Plovers* are regular migrants and winter visitors, and occasional *Dunlins* can be found on the sandier stretches of beach. In winter, small numbers of *Brent Geese* are likely around the Causeway feeding on *Zostera* (eel-grass) seaweed, upending in the shallow reaches of the low tide or just swimming around. At this time of year *Great Northern* and *Black Throated Divers* as well as *Slavonian* and *Black Necked Grebes* should be visible all around Lihou waters, but more particularly when cold weather forces birds to flee further south.

This would also be the time to look out for Ducks, *Eiders* are not uncommon in Guernsey waters, a large duck with a distinctly heavy head, occasionally building up into small flocks. *Common Scoters* are a possibility, small dark ducks usually in parties and there is a good chance of seeing *Red Breasted Mergansers*.

The western extremes of Lihou Island are a good spot for 'sea watching', i.e. recording of birds passing offshore in spring and autumn. *Gannets* are a regular feature, performing spectacular dives in their fishing parties. *Manx Shearwaters* and *Great Skuas (Bonxies)* are likely to be seen particularly in autumn (late August to October), as are *Arctic Skuas* and flocks of *Kittiwakes* and *Terns*, both *Common* and *Sandwich Terns* have bred on the offshore islets of Guernsey, possibly on Lihoumel. When seawatching, one can at times visibly watch passerine migrations with influxes of birds passing overhead heading for Guernsey. *Swifts, Swallows* and *House Martins* might be seen, as well as many *Yellow Wagtails, Tree Pipits* and numerous Finches.

Resident birds in Lihou Island obviously include a few species of seabirds. The wintering high tide *Oystercatcher* roost on the raised storm beach which can be seen from L'Erée Head in Guernsey has been known to number in excess of five hundred birds and could be considered as the largest regular roost of this species in Guernsey waters. A few pairs of *Oystercatcher* remain to breed in Lihou, their 'Kleep, Kleep' call is a prominent feature of summer bird life. It is also believed that *Ringed Plovers* may have bred in recent years. Another high tide roost of birds visible from the coast of Guernsey is that of *Herring* and *Great Black-backed Gulls* on the higher grassy areas towards the 'spine' of the Island, indeed on visiting Lihou you can find moulted gull feathers in this area. The latter two species can be found nesting on the rocky outcrops of Lihoumel along with *Shags* and possibly the odd pair of *Cormorants* which can be seen regularly swimming and diving all around the coast. (Visiting Lihoumel, except by special arrangement, is discouraged to avoid disturbing the birds).

The passerine residents are limited to nest site availability, *House Sparrows* and *Starlings* can always be seen around the boundaries of the house. Numbers of *Starlings* can greatly increase with 'immigrants' in late autumn and winter when large visiting parties descend to feed on the *vraic* (seaweed) covered shores. *Rock Pipits* can be found all the year round, zooming about on the beaches and a close relative, the *Meadow Pipit*, is resident inland as is the *Skylark* with its parachuting display flight song, both of these species are ground nesters therefore the grassy habitat over most of the Island is ideal for them. Habitat for other passerines is provided by the bracken and brambles, housing such species as *Blackbird, Dunnock, Wren, Linnet* and *Stonechat*.

Non-breeding birds present most of the year include *Grey Herons* which can at certain times number ten or more and can be seen fishing by the Causeway or roosting on Lissroy or Lihoumel. *Curlew, Redshank* and *Turnstone* are to be found feeding in the winter months. *Kestrels* which are not thought to breed in Lihou Island will be seen hovering over the Island having flown across from Guernsey along with *Magpies* and *Carrion Crows*, even a pair of *Ravens* are regularly observed circling the Island.

Cuckoos have been recorded, breeding with the 'host parents' being *Meadow Pipits* and a few years ago it was believed that *Shelducks* could have bred in the area.

Lihou Island has a bird list numbering more than 127 species. Rare or less common ones seen include *Short Eared Owl, Peregrine, Wryneck, Nightingale, Bluethroat, Grasshopper Warbler, Melodious Warbler, Ortolan, Lapland* and *Snow Buntings* as well as regular passage migrants like *Ring Ouzels,* and waders such as Whimbrels. When visiting Lihou Island, keep your eyes open, you never know what you may see.

The Venus Pool